The Value and Limits of Rights

Rights are part of our everyday moral and political vocabulary. Yet while few would deny that rights are important, there is a great deal of disagreement about just how valuable rights are and what their proper limits ought to be. For example, some scholars and practitioners maintain that human rights are valuable because they lay down a framework of protection while at the same time leaving people ample room to lead their lives as they see fit. They are not just another way of life but instead set the boundaries to what government can or cannot do. Others, however, hold that, while important, rights are not neutral between different ways of life and hence cannot tell us what to do when different ways of life conflict. This collection breaks new ground by tackling such questions head on. The issues it covers are some of the most vital that we face today – their relevance to contemporary social and political debates cannot be overstated. The collection should appeal to political philosophers, lawyers, human rights activists and advanced undergraduate and graduate students in the arts, humanities and social sciences.

This book was published as a special issue of *Critical Review of International, Social and Political Philosophy*.

Ian O'Flynn is Senior Lecturer in Political Theory at Newcastle University, UK.

Albert Weale is Professor of Political Theory and Public Policy at University College London, UK.

The Value and Limits of Rights
Essays in Honour of Peter Jones

Edited by
Ian O'Flynn and Albert Weale

LONDON AND NEW YORK

First published 2014
by Routledge

2 Park Square, Milton Park, Abingdon, Oxfordshire OX14 4RN
711 Third Avenue, New York, NY 10017

Routledge is an imprint of the Taylor & Francis Group, an informa business

First issued in paperback 2018

Copyright © 2014 Taylor & Francis

This book is a reproduction of *Critical Review of International, Social and Political Philosophy*, vol. 15, issue 4. The Publisher requests to those authors who may be citing this book to state, also, the bibliographical details of the special issue on which the book was based.

All rights reserved. No part of this book may be reprinted or reproduced or utilised in any form or by any electronic, mechanical, or other means, now known or hereafter invented, including photocopying and recording, or in any information storage or retrieval system, without permission in writing from the publishers.

Notice:
Product or corporate names may be trademarks or registered trademarks, and are used only for identification and explanation without intent to infringe.

British Library Cataloguing in Publication Data
A catalogue record for this book is available from the British Library

ISBN 13: 978-0-415-85422-1 (hbk)
ISBN 13: 978-1-138-37788-2 (pbk)

Typeset in Times New Roman
by Taylor & Francis Books

Publisher's Note
The publisher would like to make readers aware that the chapters in this book may be referred to as articles as they are identical to the articles published in the special issue. The publisher accepts responsibility for any inconsistencies that may have arisen in the course of preparing this volume for print.

Contents

Citation information vii
Notes on contributors ix

1. Introduction: The value and limits of rights: essays in honour of Peter Jones
   Ian O'Flynn and Albert Weale 1

2. Human rights and the diversity of value
   Hillel Steiner 9

3. Grounding human rights
   David Miller 21

4. Why liberals should not worry about subsidizing opera
   John Horton 41

5. Rights as democracy
   Richard Bellamy 61

6. The right to health versus good medical care?
   Albert Weale 85

7. The value and limits of rights: a reply
   Peter Jones 107

8. Peter Jones: Publications 129

Index 133

Citation information

The chapters in this book were originally published in the *Critical Review of International, Social and Political Philosophy*, volume 15, issue 4 (September 2012). When citing this material, please use the original page numbering for each article, as follows:

Chapter 1
Introduction: The value and limits of rights: essays in honour of Peter Jones
Ian O'Flynn and Albert Weale
Critical Review of International, Social and Political Philosophy,
volume 15, issue 4 (September 2012) pp. 387–394

Chapter 2
Human rights and the diversity of value
Hillel Steiner
Critical Review of International, Social and Political Philosophy,
volume 15, issue 4 (September 2012) pp. 395–406

Chapter 3
Grounding human rights
David Miller
Critical Review of International, Social and Political Philosophy,
volume 15, issue 4 (September 2012) pp. 407–428

Chapter 4
Why liberals should not worry about subsidizing opera
John Horton
Critical Review of International, Social and Political Philosophy,
volume 15, issue 4 (September 2012) pp. 429–448

Chapter 5
Rights as democracy
Richard Bellamy

CITATION INFORMATION

Critical Review of International, Social and Political Philosophy, volume 15, issue 4 (September 2012) pp. 449–472

Chapter 6
The right to health versus good medical care?
Albert Weale
Critical Review of International, Social and Political Philosophy, volume 15, issue 4 (September 2012) pp. 473–494

Chapter 7
The value and limits of rights: a reply
Peter Jones
Critical Review of International, Social and Political Philosophy, volume 15, issue 4 (September 2012) pp. 495–516

Chapter 8
Peter Jones: Publications
Critical Review of International, Social and Political Philosophy, volume 15, issue 4 (September 2012) pp. 517–520

Please direct any queries you may have about the citations to clsuk.permissions@cengage.com

Notes on contributors

Richard Bellamy is Professor of Political Science and Director of the European Institute, University College London (UCL), University of London, UK. Recent publications include *Liberalism and Pluralism: Towards a Politics of Compromise* (Routledge, 1999), *Rethinking Liberalism* (Continuum, 2000, 2005), *Political Constitutionalism: A Republican Defence of the Constitutionality of Democracy* (Cambridge University Press, 2007) and *Citizenship: A Very Short Introduction* (Oxford University Press, 2008). He is currently working on a book with the provisional title *A Republic of European States: Cosmopolitanism, Republicanism and Democracy in the EU*.

John Horton is Professor of Political Philosophy at Keele University, UK, having previously been Director of the Morrell Studies in Toleration at the University of York, UK. He is the author of *Political Obligation* (Palgrave Macmillan, revised edition, 2010), and of numerous articles on contemporary political philosophy, especially in the fields of toleration, political obligation and, most recently, on realism in political theory.

Peter Jones is Emeritus Professor of Political Philosophy at Newcastle University, UK. He is the author of *Rights* (Macmillan, 1994) and editor, with Simon Caney and David George, of *National Rights, International Obligations* (Westview 1996), with Simon Caney, of *Human Rights and Global Diversity* (Frank Cass 2001), and of *Group Rights* (Ashgate, 2009). As well as examining various aspects of rights, his published work has also ranged over a number of other subjects, including toleration, identity, recognition, cultural diversity, discrimination law, democracy, freedom of expression, neutrality, international and global justice, and the nature of liberalism.

David Miller is Professor of Political Theory in the University of Oxford and an Official Fellow of Nuffield College. Educated at Selwyn College, Cambridge and Balliol College, Oxford, he taught at the universities of Lancaster and East Anglia before taking up his present post in 1979. He became a Fellow of the British Academy in 2002. He has a long-standing interest in questions of social justice (*Social Justice* (1976), *Principles of Social Justice*

(1999)) and in nationality and multiculturalism (*On Nationality* (1995), *Citizenship and National Identity* (2000)). Recently, he has been working on global justice, territorial rights and immigration (*National Responsibility and Global Justice* (2007)), as well as more specifically on human rights.

Ian O'Flynn is Senior Lecturer in Political Theory, Newcastle University, UK. He has held fellowships at the universities of Pennsylvania and Essex, and is a former Visiting Scholar at Harvard University. He is the author of *Deliberative Democracy and Divided Societies* (EUP, 2006) and editor, with David Russell, of *Power Sharing: New Challenges for Divided Societies* (Pluto, 2005). Broadly, his research focuses on questions concerning the nature and requirements of democracy in multicultural and multinational societies. He is currently writing papers on political integration and, with Peter Jones, on deliberative democracy and compromise.

Hillel Steiner is a Fellow of the British Academy, Emeritus Professor of Political Philosophy in the University of Manchester, Professor of Political Philosophy in the University of Salford, Research Professor in Philosophy and the Freedom Center, University of Arizona, and Research Fellow in the *Justitia Amplificata* Centre for Advanced Studies at the Goethe University of Frankfurt. He is the author of *An Essay on Rights* (Blackwell, 1994) and co-author, with Matthew Kramer and Nigel Simmonds, of *A Debate Over Rights: Philosophical Enquiries* (Oxford University Press, 1998). His current research projects include ones on the concept of 'the just price' and the application of libertarian principles to global, and to genetic, inequalities.

Albert Weale is Professor of Political Theory and Public Policy in the School of Public Policy, University College London, UK. His research has concentrated on issues of political theory and public policy, especially the theory of justice and the theory of democracy, health policy and comparative environmental policy. His principal publications include *Equality and Social Policy* (Routledge and Kegan Paul, 1978), *Political Theory and Social Policy* (Macmillan, 1983), *The New Politics of Pollution* (Manchester University Press, 1992), *Democracy* (Macmillan, 1999 and 2007 revised), *Democratic Citizenship and the European Union* (Manchester University Press, 2005) and, with others, *The Theory of Choice* (Blackwell, 1992) and *Environmental Governance in Europe* (Oxford University Press, 2000) as well as a number of edited works and papers. His latest book is *Democratic Justice and the Social Contract* (Oxford: Oxford University Press, 2013).

Introduction: The value and limits of rights: essays in honour of Peter Jones

Ian O'Flynn[a] and Albert Weale[b]

[a]*School of Geography, Politics, and Sociology, Newcastle University, Newcastle upon Tyne, UK;* [b]*Department of Political Science, School of Public Policy, University College London, London, UK*

The essays collected in this issue were written in honour of Peter Jones, Emeritus Professor of Political Philosophy at Newcastle University and one of the finest political philosophers of his generation. They are revised versions of papers first presented to him at a conference at Newcastle University in February 2010 to celebrate his then impending retirement. Along with many others in the profession, all the participants at that event hoped that, in marking his retirement from the university, they were not marking his departure from his chosen profession.

Readers of this journal will know that Jones's work over the years has been concerned with a number of issues central to normative political theory, including toleration, freedom of expression, multiculturalism, justice, state neutrality, value pluralism, the status of majority rule, the evaluation of choice, and forms of welfare and stigma. In all these fields he has brought his characteristic fluency of expression, careful balance of judgement, attention to relevant empirical issues and, above all, clarity of analysis. His achievement is all the more remarkable because the topics on which he has chosen to write are ones where assertion and obfuscation are frequently substituted for rational argument. However, if there is one field of political theory in which he is the acknowledged authority, it is the subject of rights. Not only in his book *Rights* (Jones 1994), but also in his other writings, he has carefully distinguished the wheat from the chaff in controversies surrounding this central, but contested, notion. Of course, one must always be careful in assigning labels to political philosophers or positioning them within particular camps. Yet when it comes to explaining just why it is that human rights are valuable, Jones shares much in common with thinkers in the natural rights tradition.

To be sure, the idea of natural rights has attracted much criticism. According to Jeremy Bentham, for example, 'Natural rights is simple nonsense: natural and imprescriptable rights, rhetorical nonsense, nonsense upon stilts' (Bentham 2002, p. 330). We might wish there were such rights, but rights do not exist until they have been enacted in law and placed on the statute book. Yet most of the ridicule that natural rights thinking has attracted has stemmed from a misunderstanding or a caricature of what is meant by 'natural'. The term is not meant to suggest that rights occur naturally in the world about us, as leaves grow on trees, but merely that there are certain ways in which we ought to treat or not to treat other human beings just as human beings. Hence, natural rights are 'natural' in that they apply to human beings universally or without distinction and hence are not merely artificial or man-made.

For Jones, the idea of human rights likewise supposes that there are certain ways in which any human being is entitled to be treated or not be treated. Since human rights are rights that we have simply by virtue of being human, they may be said to exist in advance of government and hence must be upheld by government. They are not merely legal rights, because legal rights are those rights that governments themselves create. Jones has consistently maintained that, as such, human rights are valuable because they lay down a framework of protection, while at the same time leaving people ample room to lead their lives as they see fit. They are not just another way of life, conception of the good or encompassing doctrine, but instead set the boundaries to what government can or cannot do. If anyone is capable of persuading us that human rights are not 'nonsense on stilts', it is Jones.

Yet, even when we are convinced of the value of the language of rights in capturing the fundamental importance of the limits of state power over individuals, there remain many problems in understanding their implications and significance. The papers in this volume take up four important issues concerned with the value and limits of rights: how logically our understanding of rights relates to various conceptions of the good; the extent to which the practice of rights can be neutral between different conceptions of the good; the extent to which rights are associated with the 'basic structure' of society involving a sharp separation between constitutional and everyday political questions; and the extent to which rights impart an individualistic bias to our thinking. The papers in this volume deal with these issues in turn.

Turning first to the question of the logical relationship between rights and conceptions of the good, there is a familiar distinction between so-called continuous and discontinuous ways of thinking. According to the continuous approach, a theory of human rights needs to be linked to particular conceptions of the good with their own distinctive metaphysical, historical or cultural ways of thought. For example, human rights might be explicated in terms of the Catholic tradition of natural law. Thus, Maritain (1943/1971) wrote that although 'strangers to Christian philosophy can have a profound and authentic feeling for the human person and his dignity' it was Christian philosophy that carried the understanding 'to a higher point of accomplishment' (pp. 4–5). Conversely, one might appeal to the Enlightenment values of emancipation (Paine 1791). In these sorts of approaches our account of rights is grounded in broader understandings of social and political life and of the place of human beings within the world. The evident difficulty with such approaches is the problem of what Rawls (1996) famously called 'reasonable pluralism', the view that given the burdens of judgement under which we all labour, there are a number of competing and incompatible conceptions of the good that can be reasonably held by people.

As a result, many political theorists have found a discontinuous way of thinking more plausible. On this discontinuous account of rights, the language of rights is not to be understood as an expression of a particular conception of the good or metaphysical doctrine. Rather it is to be understood as a way of trying to cope with doctrinal diversity in a way that is morally acceptable to all. As Jones himself expressed the fundamental thrust of human rights theory, its task

> is not to add yet another voice to that cacophony of disagreement. ... Instead, it should be concerned with how people ought to relate to one another as people with different beliefs. So its proper concern is with people who hold doctrines, rather than with the doctrines they hold. (Jones 2000, p. 37)

On this view, rights are a second-order device for ordering conflicts between people, telling us what to do when conceptions of the good conflict with one another.

In his contribution to this volume, Hillel Steiner also assumes that human rights are not just another way of life but are independent of, or discontinuous with, the disagreements they are meant to regulate. A theory of human rights is not a first-order theory that tells people how to live but a second-order order theory that tells people what to do when different ways of life conflict, as they inevitably will in any modern, pluralistic society. More specifically, human rights regulate conflict by distributing freedom: when ways of life conflict, human rights tell us who should be free to do what. Of course, if human rights distribute freedom, they themselves must be the product of a freedom-distributing rule. Steiner spends much of his paper defending what he takes to be the most plausible candidate for such a rule – one which he sees as deriving from the fundamental right to equal individual freedom and which has the properties of doctrinal neutrality and moral primacy. The point of such a rule is to generate rights that stand outside of and above the conflicts those rights are meant to regulate. In this way he seeks to show how a programme of discontinuity needs a programme of negative liberty understood in a particular way. One important question in the theory of rights is whether the universality, to which the discontinuous account of rights strives, requires commitment to a negative conception of freedom in the physicalist form that Steiner supplies.

In his contribution David Miller is more critical of the strict separation between first-order and second-order conceptions of rights and wonders whether the discontinuous strategy over-generalizes from the case of toleration. He identifies a feature of the good – meeting needs that allow people to lead a minimally decent way of life – that is sufficiently universal to form a basis for human rights. Rather than regulate conflicts between ways of life, Miller contends that the reason why we should ascribe human rights to human beings is because those rights secure our basic needs. Since basic needs are common to us all, the rights that those needs generate will not be biased in favour of some people. For these reasons, Miller suggests that human rights do not simply impose a form of life. Human rights will have the same practical force for everyone, because everyone will have much the same reasons for wanting to have his or her basic needs met. Yet at the same time, he argues that particular ways of life have an important bearing on our thinking about particular human rights. As human beings, each of us may have the same basic needs. Yet because different ways of life will rank those needs differently, there will be different views about which human rights are to have priority. Insofar as human rights vary in their application, there will be no discontinuity between how human rights are justified and the particular forms of life to which they are to apply. Their value will be partly universal, but also partly a matter of how they are perceived by different people differently situated.

In Miller's contribution, we have already started to move from the first issue – the logical connection between rights and differing conceptions of the good – to the second issue, namely how far commitment to rights requires a policy of state neutrality and what is implied if it does. In his contribution, John Horton argues that the idea of state neutrality is both implausible and unnecessary. It is implausible because appeals to such principles as freedom or equality will always mean different things to different people, depending on their way of life, even if they are universally shared at some level of abstraction. It is unnecessary because state support for a way of life need not amount to the imposition of that way of life on others. For example, the state may decide to subsidise opera from general taxation, which many liberals might regard as unfair or unjust. Yet as Horton points out, subsidising opera does not impose a way of life on others; indeed, many people may be perfectly happy to see some of their taxation go to opera, even though opera has no place in their way of life. Similarly, it need not be a wrongful violation of the principle of neutrality to have one legally established religion in a society where many religions are practised.

According to Horton, then, although one personally may have little interest in opera, one could still wish to see opera subsidised for the benefit of others. Analogously, one may think that human rights are nonsense on stilts or simply have little personal interest in them (that this attitude is possible only for those whose human rights are already secure is certainly possible), but still prefer a world in which real efforts were made to uphold those rights for others. Put another way, one might think that human rights are the reflection of a particular way of life, as Horton implies. Yet although one might therefore reject the discontinuous conception of human rights favoured by Jones, that need not commit one to the view that human rights (unfairly or unjustifiably) impose a way of life.

Rights are often seen as prior to and imposing moral limits on politics, with the implication that political institutions should be designed in such a way that, in the words of the American Declaration of Independence, 'governments are instituted' to secure rights. In practice, this claim is often taken further to imply a separation between constitutional politics and normal politics with constitutional provisions being more rigid than day-to-day legislation and involving different methods of decision-making, most notably the use of constitutional courts rather than elected legislatures, to determine when rights have been breached or the justifiable limits of governmental power over-stepped. Adopting this perspective, Jones has written that the political purpose of human rights is 'to tell those who wield political power what they may and may not do' (Jones 1994, p. 222). Significantly, the limits required by rights apply as much to democratic majorities as they do to governments. Although some rights, like the right to vote, may be required for a democracy to flourish, other rights, for example the right not to be tortured, are not only independent of majority rule, but also they may be threatened by majority rule, so that rights may need to be asserted against democracy (Jones 1994, pp. 173–175). From this point of view, rights are associated with the 'basic structure' of society in a strong sense, involving a sharp separation between constitutional and everyday political questions, the third of the issues with which this volume is concerned.

Richard Bellamy contests this distinction between constitutional politics and everyday politics, with its associated claim that issues involving rights should properly be removed from the realm of majoritarian decision-making. For Bellamy, by contrast, when understood from a pluralist perspective, democracy is the foundation of rights rather than in competition with them. When rights are asserted or claimed, this is most justifiability done when it is done in a democratic spirit. The pillars of his argument are the twin claims that the meaning and scope of rights is subject to reasonable disagreement among persons and that a fair way of resolving disagreements is through a majoritarian political process. This argument may be read as a reflexive application to questions of the right of the claim that we need a distinction between first-order and second-order accounts of the role of rights, because conceptions of the good conflict. What happens when conceptions of the right conflict? Bellamy's answer is that we can only find an answer to this question in democratic practice and an understanding of what fair competition among competing claims to the right involves.

Albert Weale tackles this concern about how the good relates to the right in a paper that evaluates the extent to which the individualistic language of there being a right to health helps in the task of determining a just allocation of medical care. With this, we arrive at the last of the four issues. As Weale points out, the claim that each of us has a human right to health is not easily squared with the claim that a good healthcare system should secure high-quality comprehensive healthcare for all, without financial barriers to access. There are, in fact, two competing logics at work. The first is deontological and stresses what each person is owed simply by virtue of his or her standing as a human being; the second is teleological and seeks to advance our common ends as members of shared way of life. How and whether these competing logics can be melded has important implications for our thinking about the value and limits of rights.

Of course, someone might say that there is no real incompatibility here. We simply see how far, or how extensively, the human right to healthcare can be realized in any given society. Yet as Weale argues, this strategy can only take us so far. There may be a human right to basic healthcare. But questions about the highest attainable levels of healthcare inevitably bring larger collective goals and purposes into play: in the light of its own way of life, each society will need to decide what resources it is willing to make available, how different priorities are to be assessed, how healthcare is to be balanced against other social goods (such as education or external defence), and so forth. As Weale makes clear, this is not to suggest that human rights have no role to play or that they are practically unimportant. But it is to suggest that once we begin to think in terms of larger social goods and purposes, the value of thinking in terms of human rights somewhat begins to fall away.

Disputes over the four central questions identified above – the relation of the right to the good, the meaning of state neutrality, the extent to which rights require a sharp separation between constitutional and everyday political questions, and the extent to which rights impart an individualistic bias to our thinking – can be placed in context if a distinction is made between a moderate and a maximum programme in relation to rights theory. The moderate thesis is that the language of rights captures an important element of any viable political morality, particularly for communities that have gone beyond adherence to the norms of a traditional and inherited political morality and are seeking for the just foundations of political order. However, there are other elements of political morality – for example, a concern with the common good or common welfare – that sometimes enter into competition with the language of rights or suggest distinctive considerations that are not captured in the language of rights. Moreover, it is not just that there is difference and competition; it is also that we may not be able to order these elements with respect to one another in a general way. From this point of view, the right is not necessarily prior to the good, the meaning of state neutrality can be flexibly interpreted, there is no sharp separation of constitutional and normal politics and we are sometimes better thinking in terms of collectively agreed purposes rather than individual rights. Rights are important, but not all important.

The maximum programme, by contrast, holds on to the thesis that, in making rights central to a political morality, we have also to commit ourselves to a set of priorities in relation to individuals, groups and the state and their place in political authority: the right is prior to the good; neutrality is prior to the pursuit of even widely shared social values; constitutional adjudication is prior to majoritarian politics; and individual rights are prior to collectively established purposes. The proponent of such a thesis may regret some of these implications from a personal or a political point of view, but from the theoretical point of view they can be seen as the logical implications of a strong claim about the values of rights.

Throughout his work, Professor Jones has insisted that we cannot in a serious political morality do without the concept of rights. In working out the implications of this fundamental claim, he has clarified what positions and possibilities are open to those who share his conviction. One implication, with which he will agree, is that others, like the authors of these papers, have the right to disagree with some, at least, of his claims.

Acknowledgements

The Editors thank Rowan Cruft for kindly agreeing to act as referee for this issue. They are grateful for his insightful comments.

References

Bentham, J., 2002. *Nonsense upon stilts or Pandora's box opened, or the French Declaration of the Rights prefixed to the constitution of 1791 laid open and exposed – with a comparative sketch of what has been done on the same subject in the constitution of 1795, and a sample of Citizen Sieyès. In*: P. Schofield, C. Pease-Watkin, and C. Blamires, eds. *Rights, representation, and reform: nonsense upon stilts and the other writings on the French Revolution*. Oxford: Clarendon, 317–401.
Jones, P., 1994. *Rights*. Basingstoke: Macmillan.
Jones, P., 2000. Human rights and diverse cultures: continuity or discontinuity? *Critical Review of International Social and Political Philosophy*, 3, 27–50.
Maritain, J., [1943] 1971. *The rights of man and natural law*. Trans. D.C. Anson. New York, NY: Gordian.
Paine, T., 1791. *Rights of man: being an answer to Mr. Burke's attack on the French Revolution*. London: J.S. Jordan.
Rawls, J., 1996. *Political liberalism*. 2nd edition. New York, NY: Columbia University Press.

Human rights and the diversity of value

Hillel Steiner

Politics, School of Social Sciences, University of Manchester, Manchester, UK

> This paper argues that the independence from intercultural disagreement, that Peter Jones attributes to human rights, implies that those rights are best understood as modelled on the Will Theory of rights and are derived from each person's foundational right to equal (negative) freedom.

Introduction

> One of the most common objections brought against human rights thinking is that we live in a world characterized by diversity of value. Theories of human rights necessarily ascribe rights universally to all humanity. Some people find that universalism implausible given the plurality of cultures, ideologies and religious beliefs to be found among human beings. Others find it objectionable. They see the assertion of human rights as an exercise in cultural (usually Western) domination or an all too convenient excuse for some states to meddle in the affairs of others. (Jones 1996, p. 183)

> [M]y argument will not show that men have any right (save the equal right of all to be free) which is 'absolute', 'indefeasible', or 'imprescriptible'. This may for many reduce the importance of my contention, but I think that the principle that all men have an equal right to be free, meagre as it may seem, is probably all that the political philosophers of the liberal tradition need have claimed to support any programme of action even if they have claimed more. (Hart 1955/1967, p. 54)

For many years now, Peter Jones's work has set the standard for scholarly excellence on the subject of rights and value pluralism. In his paper, which begins with the first passage quoted above, Jones presents a characteristically discerning — and, in my view, utterly successful — critique of John Rawls's attempt to incorporate a 'political' or 'free-standing' conception of human rights into his more general just law of peoples: a conception which would be independent of comprehensive doctrines, which would regulate conduct compliant with them, and which would therefore be 'appropriate for a society of political societies each of which has its own internal conception of justice' (Jones 1996, p. 187). As Rawls says, in *The Law of Peoples*:

> Comprehensive doctrines, religious or non-religious, might base the idea of human rights on a theological, philosophical, or moral conception of the nature of the human person. That path the Law of Peoples does not follow. What I call human rights are, as I have said, a proper subset of the rights possessed by citizens in a liberal constitutional regime, or of the rights of members of a decent hierarchical society. (Rawls 1999, p. 81)[1]

Somewhat similarly, H. L. A. Hart's aspiration, in the celebrated article from which the second opening quotation above is taken, is to advance the conception of natural rights that he finds implicit in the works of political philosophers of, specifically, the liberal tradition.[2]

My own experience of thinking about what can count as human rights has led me to the conclusion that we get a lot more mileage out of staring at the word 'rights' than by staring at the word 'human'. The aim of this paper is to suggest that Hart's account more successfully accomplishes what Rawls aspires but fails to do, and what Jones convincingly argues is needed by any plausible theory of human rights. And it does so by virtue of the general *concept of rights* that it deploys.

Doctrinal neutrality

In thinking about what our basic moral rights are, both Hart and, more arguably, Rawls deploy what Jones, following Ronald Dworkin, has identified as the *discontinuous strategy*. 'A continuous strategy would try to establish a continuity between the theory of human rights and the various doctrines to which people are committed' (Jones 2001, p. 34). But, as Jones persuasively demonstrates, if the kind of global moral consensus thereby required as the grounding for such a theory actually existed, it would be very difficult to find a conceptual space for human rights at all. At best, such theories would merely re-describe that pre-existing moral consensus in the language of human rights.

Accordingly, recourse must be had to the discontinuous approach.

> The strategy of discontinuity aims to develop liberal principles which are categorically different from, and which are justified independently of, the conceptions of the good whose pursuit they are designed to regulate (Jones 1995, p. 516). We are supposing that diversity of belief and value is a normal part of the human condition. ... Given that state of affairs, we can look to a theory of human rights to provide for that diversity rather than simply add to it. ... The task of a theory of human rights is not to add yet another voice to that cacophony of disagreement. Its task is to provide for a world in

which there is that disagreement. But it is to provide for that world not by itself entering the lists of doctrinal controversy and attempting to declare which doctrine is true and which false. ... Instead, it should be concerned with how people ought to relate to one another as people with different beliefs. So its proper concern is with people who hold doctrines, rather than with the doctrines that they hold. (Jones 2001, p. 37)

And, from this, Jones infers that a theory of human rights can best be modelled by distinguishing different *levels* of concern, whereby doctrines and the disagreements they generate constitute the first level of concern, while the theory of human rights 'places itself outside and above the arena of doctrinal disagreement and seeks only to regulate people's relations with one another given that they have to live in that arena of disagreement' (Jones 2001, pp. 37–38). The level of concern inhabited by human rights theory – a level 'outside' and discontinuously removed from the one occupied by the cacophonous arena of doctrinal disagreement or rival conceptions of the good – is thus one where persons' moral entitlements are determined without essential reference to the comparative merit of the doctrinal commitments conflictually pursued in that arena. So how *are* those entitlements to be characterized?

One part of the answer is to be found by reflecting on the question centrally addressed in Hart's famous lectures, *Law, Liberty and Morality*, where he asks:

Is it morally permissible to enforce morality as such? ... [I]t is plain that the question is one *about* morality, but it is important to observe that it is also a question *of* morality. It is the question whether the enforcement of morality is morally justified; so morality enters into the question in two ways. (Hart 1963, pp. 4, 17)[3]

Or, as Jones might say, on two levels. For Hart's deployment of a discontinuous strategy rests upon the necessary truth that, whatever may be the set of moral rules under consideration for enforcement, a moral rule concerning their enforcement cannot be a member of that set.[4] *A fortiori*, then, it cannot be a member of that set if the very membership of that set is itself a matter of doctrinal disagreement. The content of enforcement rules – the grounds on which some conduct is enforced – must be independent of the moral status of that conduct: it must be doctrinally *neutral*. How is this possible?

Consider the characteristic function of rights in our practical thinking.[5] Their familiar role is that of items invoked in what can be called *adversarial circumstances*. What are adversarial circumstances? Well, one feature of them is certainly *disagreement*. If all of us always and everywhere agreed on what would be the best thing to do in any particular situation, it looks pretty undeniable that rights would quickly disappear from our language. If you and I and everyone else all agreed on the most appropriate destination for my latest salary increment – whether it be a particular charity or the Inland Revenue or my bank account – any talk about who has what rights with respect to that increment would be utterly superfluous.

But disagreement is only a necessary, not a sufficient, condition of adversarial circumstances. The sufficient condition is what I call *deadlock*. Suppose I disagree with the coach of the New York Yankees about the fielding strategy to be pursued when the bases are loaded and there is a fairly mediocre hitter up to bat. This is *not* an adversarial circumstance, though it is one of disagreement. It is not an adversarial one because there is nothing I can actually *do* to stop the coach's strategy from being deployed. It would be different – it *would be* adversarial – if, say, I were the Yankees' second-base man. Then I *could* escalate my disagreement into deadlock by refusing to deploy the coach's strategy and doing something else instead. Broadly speaking, then, deadlock occurs when two disagreeing persons' chosen courses of action *intersect*: that is, when what each proposes to do or have done would preclude the occurrence of what the other proposes. Their two courses of action are jointly unperformable or what I have elsewhere called *incompossible* (cf. Steiner 1994, pp. 33–41, 86–101, 190–194, Steiner 1998, pp. 262–274).

It is in these circumstances that people begin to think about ringing up their solicitors to consult them about their rights. Of course, before they start reaching for their rights, each will presumably try to convince the other that his or her own proposed action is the better of the two. And sometimes, perhaps often, one of these attempts at persuasion will succeed. If it does succeed, *it eliminates the deadlock by eliminating the disagreement*. Presumably, if the coach and the second-base man share the same dominant aim – say, winning the game – a sufficiently detailed scrutiny of various bits of empirical data will result in one of them changing his mind and backing off. But what if two adversaries cannot eliminate their disagreement? What if, agreeing on all the pertinent facts, they nevertheless do not share that aim or, even if they do, they do not prioritize it in the same way in relation to their other aims?

It is here, I think, that reflection on who has what rights really comes into its own. For the distinctive function of such thinking is to secure the elimination of deadlocks *without* eliminating the disagreements that generate them. Rights supply adversaries with reasons to back off from interference, when they have no other reason to allow the performance of the actions they are interfering with. One of the two contending adversaries becomes a (disapproving) observer of the other's conduct. The second-base man need concur with neither the coach's dominant aim nor the fielding strategy motivated by it in order consistently to acknowledge the coach's right that he comply with that strategy.

If this suggestion is correct, if it accurately reflects a salient aspect of how we commonly think about rights, then – abstract and general as it admittedly is – one important inference that we can draw from it is this: the general content of such rights is not determined by any of the aims/priorities motivating the disagreement between the adversarial parties. For, *ex hypothesi*, they have already been down the road of searching for a consensus on these commitments, and have returned empty-handed. Their own values do not supply either of them with sufficient reasons to do the requisite backing off. So if appeals to rights are going to do any work in resolving their deadlock, without falsely presupposing the absence of their disagreement, the general content of those rights has to be (in some sense) *independent* of the content of adversaries' competing commitments.

This claim, of the content-independence of rights, should not be read as implying an absence of disagreement over that content: there clearly can be, and is, such disagreement. Rather, what that claim implies is (only) that, whatever rival views of that content there may be, those views are not respectively aligned with, or derived from, the aims or priorities or doctrinal commitments that are in mutual contention and that rights are meant to adjudicate. That said, however, I shall presently advance an argument concerning the sorts of rights content that are ruled out by this adjudicative conception of the function of rights.

The job of rights, then, is to demarcate *domains* – spheres of practical choice within which the choices made by designated individuals (and groups) must not be subjected to interference – and to specify those demarcations without reference to the content of the choices to be made within those spheres. It thus requires no very extended argument to show that rights, so conceived, amount to *normative allocations of freedom*. They reserve parts of the world to their owners' discretion (which may well be partially governed by their owners' doctrinal commitments) and they imply that, within those domains, such changes (or continuities) in the state of the world as those owners choose to occur must not be obstructed by others.[6] Those others bear duties to refrain from such obstruction.

This construal of rights as freedom allocations is sufficient to explain why those duties are uncontroversially seen as permissibly *enforceable*. For, putting the matter as broadly as possible, we can say that to prevent someone's chosen disposition of elements within his or her domain is to diminish that person's allotted freedom: specifically, it makes that person unfree to secure whatever is aimed at in that disposition. A set of rights-creating rules that lacked provision for the enforcement of those duties – that allowed, much less required, rights violations to stand unprevented or unreversed – could not then consistently be described as doing what it purports to do: namely, assigning that discretionary domain to that person. 'No right without a remedy', as the legal maxim says.

Now it is evidently no great imaginative leap to substitute the contentious inhabitants of Jones's arena of disagreement for the Yankees' coach and second-base man. The diversity of their respective sets of doctrinal commitments, and the possible absence of any 'overlapping consensus' between those sets, are precisely what create the conceptual space for human rights as Jones has characterized them. Those rights inhabit a level removed from the doctrinal disagreement-arena, and are relevantly invocable only when that arena's inhabitants threaten, literally, to get in one another's way. And when they *are* invoked, they are not called upon to supply answers to questions of the form: Which one of these two incompossible courses of action is morally better, services more vital human interests, delivers greater social utility, etc.? For these are questions which can be answered only doctrinally and, *ex hypothesi*, the disputants have already addressed them and have remained in disagreement over either the correct answers to them or, more likely, the weight attached to those questions themselves. Rather, the question posed by the invocation of rights is: Which one of these disputants should have the *freedom* to pursue his or her chosen course of action? And this is a question which can be answered only by reference to some rule that distributes freedom, and that does so without regard to the doctrinal credentials of whatever actions constitute the exercise of that freedom.

Moral primacy

In addition to that doctrinal neutrality, a freedom-distributing rule also possesses the other attribute which Jones ascribes to human rights: namely, that they stand 'above' the doctrinal disagreement-arena and 'regulate' the actions that disputants can permissibly take in pursuit of their contending commitments. In other words, moral rights enjoy a *primacy* status in our moral reasoning.

Although the assignment of this status to moral rights has not gone unchallenged, it does seem to conform to widely held views. Such an assignment does, for instance, appear to be a necessary condition for making sense of the common notion of 'having a right to do wrong' (cf. Waldron 1981). Of course, and following Hohfeld, no one can ever be strictly said to have a *right* to do anything: at most, persons have *liberties* to act, and having a liberty to do something does not itself entail a duty in anyone else. But we can have rights – Hohfeldian claims – that others not interfere with our acting in certain ways, and those persons would thereby hold correlative duties of non-interference. Among the ways of acting that are protected by such claims may be ones which, in certain circumstances, are wrong on grounds other than disregard for rights.

Thus, one of morality's primary rules or values may well be *charity* – a norm which vests me with duties to transfer some of my resources to those more in need of them than I am. Assuming that I am justly entitled to those resources – that I hold moral rights that others not interfere with my disposition of them – this does *not* entail that I do no wrong in refusing to act charitably and insist on withholding those resources from needier persons. All that is entailed by assigning primacy to moral rights, is that others would be committing a *worse* wrong by forcing me to make that transfer. In other words, morality's assigning such primacy entails that the following three alternatives are listed in descending order of moral desirability: (1) my choosing to transfer my resources to the needy; (2) my withholding those resources; and (3) my attempting to withhold those resources but being forced by others to transfer them. It is outcome (2) that represents having (i.e. exercising) a right to do wrong. The fact that my withholding is an exercise of my rights is insufficient morally to justify that act. All that it would suffice to justify are whatever actions might be necessary to prevent or remedy my being forced to transfer (cf. Steiner 1996).

There is another, and previously noted, feature of our moral thinking that suggests primacy status for moral rights. In everyday moral discussions, we standardly do not invoke rights to resolve our disagreements except as a last resort. Thus, as members of a newspaper's editorial staff, we might disagree with one another about which candidate the paper should support in a current electoral contest. Typically, the way we would argue about the relative merits of each of the candidates is by ascertaining facts, clarifying conceptual ambiguities and appealing to one or another of the more fundamental moral rules or values that might severally be associated with each alternative. In other words, we would do our best to reach a consensus on which option is the morally optimal one. It is only when we find ourselves unable to reach that consensus that I might fall back on asserting 'Look, I'm the managing editor here – I'm the one with the moral right to decide whom the paper supports'. For me to offer that argument at the *outset* of our discussion would be not only churlish but also beside the point, since what that discussion is about is how best I can exercise my right: that it *is* my right is not in dispute. The resolving role of moral rights in moral disputes is not to dissolve disagreement but rather to determine *who* – in the face of indissoluble disagreement – is rightfully empowered to decide what is to be done. And it seems clear that moral rights can play this adjudicating role only if their status is one of having priority over whatever other moral norms may be in mutual contention in such disputes.

Equal freedom

So, what is the content of the freedom-distributing rule that generates human rights with the two Jonesian properties of doctrinal neutrality and moral primacy, of being *outside* and *above* the disagreement-arena? Hart, as that opening quotation indicates, believes it to be one distributing entitlements to freedom *equally* (cf. Miller 2012). And Jones concurs, remarking that 'faced with first-level differences of belief, a theory of human rights should extend equal freedom to people to live according to their beliefs'

(Jones 2001, pp. 45–46). Indeed, the claim that what is ordained by basic moral rights (or justice) is an interpersonal distribution of freedom – and, moreover, an *equal* one – has a long and distinguished pedigree in political philosophy (cf. Locke 1967, pp. 287–289, Kant 1965, pp. 35–39, Spencer 1851, ch. VI, George 1931, ch. IX, Gewirth 1978, p. 3, Pollock 1981, ch. 1).[7] In the light of what has been said about neutrality, this is very much to be expected. For whereas a rule distributing X equally can be logically determinate – can be complied with, without further interpretation – a rule distributing X *un*equally cannot. That is, it cannot be determinate in the absence of a supplementary criterion that selects some unequally possessed personal attribute in proportion to which that X is to be correspondingly distributed. But no such attribute is available to do this particular supplementing job, for neither persons' neediness nor their productivity nor their virtue nor their desert – to say nothing of their religious, racial, and gender attributes – can serve this purpose *in a doctrinally neutral way*. None of them, nor any others, can be used to determine the amount of freedom to which disagreement-arena inhabitants are each entitled, without falsely presupposing the absence of their disagreement.

On this subject of determinacy, Jones does, it is true, remark that the claim that human rights vest individuals with a right to equal freedom

> may leave room for different possibilities in how precisely we define each person's domain of equal freedom. Many of those who found themselves on different sides in the Rushdie Affair were not in dispute over whether people should enjoy freedom of belief; they disagreed only over the proper make-up of each person's domain of freedom. (Jones 2001, p. 46)

I myself am uncertain as to whether this is so. Much here depends on the precise contours of our conception of freedom and, thence, on whether the domains of freedom that rights bestow on us can be compossible, if they include uncontracted rights against such irreducibly intensionally defined acts as offensive speech. For it is clear that any set of rights yielding contradictory judgements about the permissibility of a particular act either is unrealizable or (what comes to the same thing) must be modified to be realizable.[8] Be this as it may, it remains true that only a right to equal freedom can possess both the doctrinal neutrality and the moral primacy that Jones regards as essential for human rights.

Now, to conceive of rights as entitlements to freedom – as entitlements to determine whether some change (or continuity) in the state of the world must or need not occur – is to embrace the Will Theory of rights, a theory of which Hart is the leading modern exponent and which his 1955 essay on natural rights is commonly taken to exemplify (cf. MacCormick 1981, p. 149, Steiner 2008, *passim*). In a deservedly famous passage from his classic statement of that theory, he identifies the fundamental structural components of the sort of discretionary domain sketched above. Since the existence of enforceable duties is an uncontested condition for the existence of rights, Hart suggests that these components are best understood as the several ingredients jointly constituting the *control* that one person can have over the duty of another:

> In the area of conduct covered by that duty the individual who has the right is a small-scale sovereign to whom the duty is owed. The fullest measure of control comprises three distinguishable elements: (i) the right holder may waive or extinguish the duty or leave it in existence; (ii) after breach or threatened breach of duty he may leave it 'unenforced' or may 'enforce' it by suing for compensation or, in certain cases, for an injunction or mandatory order to restrain the continued or further breach of duty; and (iii) he may waive or extinguish the obligation to pay compensation to which the breach gives rise. (Hart 1982, pp. 183–184)

These ingredients of control are each Hohfeldian *powers*. And the singular clarifying service rendered by this account is to have distilled the few basic forms, that all powers assume, from their myriad contents in any given set of rules. All powers can be exhaustively classified under one or another of these basic forms. It is the possession of these powers that endows their possessor, Blue, with a discretionary domain in the following sense. Where Red owes Blue a duty to do the act A, Blue has two options: (1) that the change (or continuity) in the state of the world implied by A's occurrence – or, in the event of Red's breach, by the occurrence of Red's remedial act – is deontically necessary or required; or (2) that this change (or continuity) is deontically unnecessary or indifferent, i.e. that both its occurrence and non-occurrence are options for Red and neither is required. Will Theory rights confer freedoms on their holders by giving them the powers to demand/enforce or, alternatively, to waive performance of the entailed duty-acts correlatively owed to them.

As was indicated near the outset of this paper, Hart's natural rights essay develops the 'free-standing' or 'political' character of such rights by focusing on these conceptual properties of moral rights themselves.

> [T]he concept of a right belongs to that branch of morality which is specifically concerned to determine when one person's freedom may be limited by another's. ... Kant, in the *Rechtslehre*, discusses the obligations which arise in this branch of morality under the title of *officia juris*, 'which do not require that respect for duty shall be of itself the determining principle of the will', and contrasts them with *officia virtutis*, which have no moral worth unless done for the sake of the moral principle. His point is, I think, that we must distinguish from the rest of morality those principles regulating the proper distribution of human freedom which alone make it morally legitimate for one human being to determine by his choice how another should act. ... And it is I think a very important feature of a moral right that the possessor of it is conceived as having a moral justification for limiting the freedom of another and that he has this justification not because the action he is entitled

to require of another has some moral quality but simply because in the circumstances a certain distribution of human freedom will be maintained if he by his choice is allowed to determine how that other shall act.
(Hart 1955/1967, pp. 55–56)

When an appeal goes up, from the cacophonous arena of doctrinal disagreement to the court of human rights, what the appellants are *not* allowed to submit to that court are briefs detailing the virtues of their own doctrinal commitments and the defects of those of their opponents. Such briefs are simply irrelevant to the decision on who has the entitlement – the rightful power – to determine which of the opposing courses of action should be allowed to proceed. All that is relevant are arguments to show which appellant's being vested with that power is consonant with an equal distribution of freedom.

It follows fairly readily from this that the traditionally opposed conception of rights – the Interest Theory of rights – is incapable of sustaining such a brief. That theory's central tenet is that the necessary and sufficient condition of one person's duty's being a correlative one – of its implying another person's right – is that its fulfilment can generally be expected to serve that latter person's important interests. As such, it is beset by the insurmountable difficulty that what is in a person's interests is an object of doctrinal determination. Is it in my interest to wear a crash-helmet when driving a motorcycle? Or to refrain from eating meat on Fridays? Or to be denied the service of voluntary euthanasia? Or to refuse a lifesaving blood transfusion? Or to undergo circumcision? These, and countless other questions, can be answered only by reference to doctrines inhabiting the disagreement-arena. Accordingly, it is not those answers that can inform the ruling of the aforesaid court. Even more disabling, of any human rights court that conceived of those rights along Interest Theory lines, would be cases where two (or more) persons' undisputedly important interests cannot be jointly served. And in that regard, Jeremy Waldron, an Interest Theorist, acknowledges that 'if rights are understood along the lines of the Interest Theory ... then conflicts of rights must be regarded as more or less inevitable' (Waldron 1989, p. 503). Accordingly, rights must be understood in Will Theory terms – as entitlements to freedom – if human rights courts are to be appropriately empowered to adjudicate on disputes arising in the arena of doctrinal disagreement.

Elsewhere, I have tried to display the sorts of right that are immediately derivable from a basic right to equal freedom (cf. Steiner 1994, chs 7–8). This is not the place to rehearse that rather lengthy account. Suffice it to say, by way of a conclusion, that only this right, and the rights consonant with it, appear capable of satisfying the conditions of neutrality and primacy, which Jones has correctly identified as necessary conditions for any plausible theory of human rights.

Acknowledgements

This paper was originally presented at a conference in honour of Professor Peter Jones, entitled 'The Value and Limits of Rights', Newcastle University, Newcastle upon Tyne, UK, February 2010.

Notes

1. Jones's (1996) critique is actually aimed at Rawls's (1993) paper, also entitled 'The law of peoples', that anticipates the account subsequently advanced in his book of that title.
2. For the purposes of this paper, whatever distinction may exist between the idea of human rights and that of natural rights is of no immediate importance. Jones (1994) notes that
    > Historically the idea of human rights descended from that of natural rights. Indeed some theorists recognise no difference between them; they regard 'natural' and 'human' as merely different labels for the same kind of right. Others are less happy with that simple conflation and, while acknowledging the historical link between the two sorts of right, want to free human rights from some of the features traditionally associated with natural rights. (p. 72)

    Hart's paper does indeed eschew those traditional features.
3. Neil MacCormick has rightly suggested that Hart's natural rights essay forms the justifying ground of his liberal critique of legal moralism in *Law, Liberty and Morality* (MacCormick 1981, p. 150).
4. This, because the contrary proposal – that an enforcement rule *is* a member of that set – generates an infinite regress: that the enforcement rule becomes one of the rules to be enforced, under the auspices of a second-order enforcement rule which, in turn, becomes ..., etc.
5. The next few paragraphs are largely taken from Steiner (1998, pp. 236–238).
6. Which is *not* to imply that such conduct (changes or continuities) as owners choose to occur within their domains is therefore permissible on other (non-rights-based) grounds. Our Yankee second-base man's acknowledgement, of the rights-based permissibility of his coach's fielding strategy and of his own duty not to obstruct it, is perfectly consistent with his adamant insistence on other grounds that it is the wrong thing to do.
7. Rawls (1971) famously offers 'equal basic liberty' as lexically prime among the *several* rules constitutive of his conception of justice. Steiner (1987, pp. 55–59) argues that an important premise of Nozick's theory of just holdings (Nozick 1974) implicitly invokes something like the equal freedom rule. Sidgwick (1963, pp. 274–278) supplies a critical discussion of the claim that justice prescribes a right to equal freedom.
8. For an argument that casts doubt on the compossibility – joint performability – of duties to perform actions the descriptions of which are not reducible to extensional terms, see Steiner (1994, pp. 86–101) and Steiner (1998, pp. 262–274). The incompossibility of a set of duties implies the incompossibility of the rights they correlatively entail; there is no possible world in which all of those rights are respected.

References

George, H., 1931. *Social problems*. London: Henry George Foundation.
Gewirth, A., 1978. *Reason and morality*. Chicago, IL: University of Chicago Press.
Hart, H. L. A., 1963. *Law, liberty and morality*. Oxford: Oxford University Press.

Hart, H. L. A., [1955] 1967. Are there any natural rights? *In*: A. Quinton, ed. *Political philosophy*. Oxford: Oxford University Press; repr. from Hart, H. L. A., 1955. Are there any natural rights? *Philosophical Review*, 64, 175–191.
Hart, H. L. A., 1982. *Essays on Bentham: jurisprudence and political theory*. Oxford: Oxford University Press, ch. VII.
Jones, P., 1994. *Rights*. Houndmills: Palgrave.
Jones, P., 1995. Two conceptions of liberalism, two conceptions of justice. *British Journal of Political Science*, 25, 515–550.
Jones, P., 1996. International human rights: philosophical or political? *In*: S. Caney, D. George, and P. Jones, eds. *National rights, international obligations*. Boulder, CO: Westview, 183–204.
Jones, P., 2001. Human rights and diverse cultures. *In*: S. Caney and P. Jones, eds. *Human rights and global diversity*. London: Frank Cass, 27–50.
Kant, I., 1965. *The metaphysical elements of justice*, ed. J. Ladd. Indianapolis, IN: Bobbs-Merrill.
Locke, J., 1967. *Two treatises of government*, ed. P. Laslett. Cambridge: Cambridge University Press.
MacCormick, N., 1981. *H.L.A. Hart*. London: Edward Arnold.
Miller, D., 2012. Grounding human rights. *Critical Review of International Social and Political Philosophy*, 15 (4), 407–427.
Nozick, R., 1974. *Anarchy, state and utopia*. Oxford: Blackwell.
Pollock, L., 1981. *The freedom principle*. Buffalo, NY: Prometheus.
Rawls, J., 1971. *A theory of justice*. Cambridge, MA: Harvard University Press.
Rawls, J., 1993. The law of peoples. *In*: S. Shute and S. Hurley, eds. *On human rights: The Oxford Amnesty Lectures 1993*. New York, NY: Basic, 41–82.
Rawls, J., 1999. *The law of peoples*. Cambridge, MA: Harvard University Press.
Sidgwick, H., 1963. *The methods of ethics*. 7th edition. London: Macmillan.
Spencer, H., 1851. *Social statics*. London: John Chapman.
Steiner, H., 1987. Capitalism, justice and equal starts. *Social Philosophy and Policy*, 5, 49–71.
Steiner, H., 1994. *An essay on rights*. Oxford: Blackwell.
Steiner, H., 1996. Duty-free zones. *Aristotelian Society Proceedings*, 96, 231–244.
Steiner, H., 1998. Working rights. *In*: M. Kramer, N. Simmonds, and H. Steiner, eds. *A debate over rights: philosophical enquiries*. Oxford: Oxford University Press, 233–301.
Steiner, H., 2008. Are there *still* any natural rights? *In*: M. Kramer, C. Grant, B. Colburn and A. Hatzistavrou, eds. *The legacy of H.L.A. Hart: legal, political, and moral philosophy*. Oxford: Oxford University Press, 239–250.
Waldron, J., 1981. A right to do wrong. *Ethics*, 92, 21–39.
Waldron, J., 1989. Rights in conflict. *Ethics*, 99, 503–519.

Grounding human rights

David Miller

Nuffield College, University of Oxford, Oxford, UK

> This paper examines the idea of human rights, and how they should be justified. It begins by reviewing Peter Jones's claim that the purpose of human rights is to allow people from different cultural backgrounds to live together as equals, and suggests that this by itself provides too slender a basis. Instead it proposes that human rights should be grounded on human needs. Three difficulties with this proposal are considered. The first is the problem of whether needs are sufficiently objective for this purpose, to which it responds by drawing a distinction between human needs proper and societal needs. The second is the problem of overshoot: human needs are more expansive than human rights. It responds to this by arguing that where needs conflict, we make trade-offs before specifying the optimum set of human rights. The third is the problem of undershoot: needs cannot be used to ground civil and political rights. Here it suggests that some of these rights can be grounded directly in needs, others can be justified instrumentally, and yet others grounded in the human need for recognition. Finally the paper returns to Jones, and asks which approach to human rights is better able to justify them within both liberal and non-liberal cultures.

The problem of identifying and justifying human rights is one that Peter Jones addressed on several occasions with his customary lucidity and precision. It occupies several chapters of his book on rights, and he returned to it around five years later in the form of several articles written while he held a Nuffield Foundation fellowship (Jones 1999, 2000a, 2000b). I think it is fair to say, though, that the question he returned to was not quite the one that he had originally tackled, because in the meantime he had so to speak 'discovered culture'. That is, the main problem in the book is to find a justificatory foundation for human rights in the form of a value that can be used to underpin the range of specific human rights that we would normally wish to recognize, and what he gives us is an exemplary critical survey of the various foundations that have been suggested – moral agency, autonomy, self-ownership, needs, and so forth – which concludes that none of these can do all of the work required of it. What we might call the culturalist challenge is discussed in the last main chapter of the book, and his concluding response to it is fairly robust: 'a doctrine of human rights cannot give its blessing to practices that it identifies as morally grotesque and inhuman merely because those practices are shrouded in the mantle of culture' (Jones 1994, p. 220).

In his later articles, by contrast, he takes the problem of cultural diversity more seriously. By the problem of cultural diversity I mean simply the problem posed by the fact that human rights are supposed to be universal in scope, to apply to all societies in the contemporary world, whereas some of those societies have cultures that appear to be hostile, if not to the very idea of human rights, at least to some of the rights that appear in the usual list. If this appearance is correct, then we seem to face a fairly stark choice between the value of cultural integrity, allowing people to live according to their own culturally specific norms and conceptions of the good life, and the value of protecting human rights. In his book *Rights* (1994), Jones begins by making some conciliatory moves which have the effect of making the conflict seem less sharp, but the bottom line, as the quotation above shows, is that where conflict is unavoidable, human rights trump the claims of culture.

In his later essays, however, Jones suggests a different approach, one that takes the fact of cultural diversity as something to be built in to the theory of human rights itself. As he puts it

> both the foundation and the content of a theory of human rights has to be of a kind that makes sense against a background of diversity. But we can ask for more than that; we can also require that it should provide for that diversity. (Jones 2000a, p. 33)

So how is that to be done? His answer is that we need to be clear about the status of a theory of human rights, about the kind of theory that it is. He argues that it must be seen as a 'second-level' theory that does not operate on the same terrain as first-order theories that tell us how human life ought to be lived. Instead, its function is to regulate interactions between people who hold rival first-order views. Or, as he puts it, 'accepting the fact of first-level disagreement, it tells us how individuals should relate to one another as individuals who are caught up in first-level disagreement' (Jones 2000a, p. 38). Now if that is what a theory of human rights is supposed to be doing, this will have a big impact on issues both of justification and of substance. The justificatory question is going to be something like 'what rights must we ascribe to each person if they are going to live together as equals in a world in which they disagree radically on first-level questions about the meaning of life and so forth?' And the substantive answer is going to be that the rights we ascribe to them will primarily be the rights that allow them to live according to their own culturally specific beliefs. To cite Jones again,

> set in the context of a world in which people have different and conflicting beliefs about how they should live, [a theory of human rights] most readily issues in the prescription that each person should be free to live according to his or her beliefs. (Jones 2000a, p. 38)

This view about the nature and purpose of human rights is quite radical when set against more familiar accounts, including indeed the one that Jones takes up in *Rights*: 'the traditional political purpose of natural or human or fundamental rights has been to tell those who wield political power what they may and may not do' (Jones 1994, p. 222). The effect of the change is to make the doctrine of human rights into something like a doctrine of toleration. The revised theory may well be able to explain some rights on the standard list, for example rights that protect freedom of conscience and freedom of expression. It is much less clear how it will explain the list of socioeconomic rights – rights to subsistence, housing, healthcare and so forth. It is not even clear that it can easily explain rights connected to legal procedure such as equality before the law, or the right to a fair trial. Violations of these rights seem to have nothing directly to do with people who hold one set of cultural beliefs attempting to impose these on people who think differently, which according to the revised theory it is the purpose of human rights to prevent. Of course it is possible to take a revisionist view about the substance of human rights. But the revision here is pretty radical, and not one that I am inclined to accept. So I am not convinced that the position Jones adopts in his later essays responds to the fact of cultural diversity in the right way, at least so far as human rights are concerned.

On the other hand, I believe that he is right about two things: first that a theory of human rights does have to take the fact of cultural diversity seriously, and second that such a theory has to start by asking what the role or purpose of human rights actually is. This, I should stress, is not the way most people think about human rights: they suppose that people just *have* human rights, and do not ask the question why we should *ascribe* these rights to human beings. My disagreement with Jones, therefore, concerns not the question he asks, but the answer that he gives, which as I have said comes close to making human rights into a theory of inter-cultural toleration: human rights set out the terms under which people who inhabit diverse cultures can live together on terms of equality.

On the alternative view that I wish to defend, the purpose of a doctrine of human rights is to specify a global minimum that people everywhere, regardless of societal membership or cultural affiliation, are owed as a matter of justice. They are owed this in the first place by those who wield power in the places they are living – by their governments, in the normal case. But if for some reason the local power-holders are unable or unwilling to deliver this minimum set of entitlements, then responsibility will fall on people and governments in other countries to overcome the deficiency.[1] Thus a theory of human rights must be able to explain why people in rich countries have obligations of justice with respect to global poverty, or why outsiders may have such obligations when a country is hit by a natural disaster. It must also be able to explain why humanitarian intervention may be justified to prevent governments or other power-holders systematically violating the human rights of their subjects. In other words, the theory of human rights must identify moral claims that are powerful enough to impose potentially demanding obligations on agents who are sometimes only loosely connected to the claimants themselves, and also to override the sovereignty of established governments in certain cases. This establishes the justificatory hurdle that has to be crossed if the theory is to succeed. Moreover the theory must take cultural diversity into account precisely because it forms the basis of a pattern of rights and obligations between people who may belong to diverse cultures. So it cannot be partisan: it cannot justify rights by appeal to reasons that only have practical force for people who belong to one particular culture.

How, then, should such a theory be constructed? One popular approach is the 'overlapping consensus' strategy, which seeks to justify human rights by finding separate justifications for the same set of rights from within each cultural world-view. In other words, human rights can have multiple foundations, and the reasons we give to justify them to any given person will depend on the cultural background that he or she comes from. Like Jones, I reject this approach, for reasons that he articulates superbly well in an earlier volume of the journal, and I am just going to set it aside here (Jones 2000a, pp. 34–37).[2]

The alternative is to look for grounds for human rights that transcend particular cultures, in the sense of being available to people regardless of their cultural affiliation. We might describe this approach as attempting to justify human rights by appeal to universal human interests, interests that everyone will recognize whatever culture they belong to. The question, of course, is whether there are any such interests. This general approach subdivides into two: the grounding of human rights may be either monistic or pluralistic. Either one tries to find a way of characterizing universal human interests that can ground all of the human rights one wants to support, or else one gives up that attempt and recognizes a plurality of grounding features, each yielding a different set of rights. Although Jones does not explicitly endorse pluralism in his book, the tenor of his argument points in that direction, as he considers how a range of different possible grounds can support specific human rights.[3] Pluralistic approaches may initially seem attractive, since it may seem to strengthen human rights to give them multiple sources of support rather than to rely on a particular ground which may fail to justify some important rights that we would want to include on a canonical list.[4] But there are two corresponding dangers. One is that the failure to provide a single, coherent rationale for human rights may weaken their ethical force, since they will begin to look more like a rag-bag of claims that we are defending on quite different grounds (and what if the grounds should conflict?). The other, which is particularly germane to the present discussion, is that if we want the theory of human rights to be non-partisan, in the sense explained above, we are going to have to check, in the case of each of the grounds that we put forward, that it is accessible from within the different cultures to be found in the contemporary world. That is quite a tall order. Indeed it seems to me quite unlikely that all of the justifications for human rights that Jones considers in his book are going to pass that test. It is hard to think that self-ownership, for example, as a ground for human rights is going to have much appeal outside of societies with strongly liberal cultures. The same applies to individual autonomy as a justifying ground. So pluralism may lead us in the direction of rival, though intersecting, lists of human rights, which I assume is not a welcome outcome.

It is better, therefore, to aim for a monistic theory of human rights, so long as we can find a justifying ground that (1) delivers a sufficiently extensive list of human rights, and (2) is non-partisan, in the sense of providing a justification that people from all cultures have reason to accept. My own candidate for such a theory is human need, and in the remainder of this essay I want to sketch such a theory and defend it against certain objections, including those canvassed by Jones (1994, ch. 7).

There seem to me to be three main obstacles to overcome if we want to ground human rights on human needs – ground in the sense just explained. The first is to show that the foundation is sufficiently solid. Our aim is to be able to settle controversies about human rights, and we cannot do this if statements about human needs are equally controversial. They must be objective in the sense that they can be justified to people coming from different cultures and holding different conceptions of the good life. The second obstacle might be called the problem of overshoot. Human needs might appear to be too expansive to serve as a basis for human rights. We cannot have a human right that each of our needs is satisfied, if human rights are going to serve the political purposes that I sketched above. Meeting human needs may be a sufficiently weighty goal to ground human rights, but it appears to take us beyond human rights themselves, indeed possibly to constitute a complete, albeit somewhat utopian, political morality. The third problem is the mirror image of the second – the problem of undershoot. It might appear that needs can serve to justify *some* important human rights, but not others. We can explain why rights to food, shelter, and medical aid are human rights by appeal to the human needs they correspond to, but it is harder to do this in the case of civil and political rights such as the right to vote. The problem of undershoot might lead us back in the direction of a pluralistic theory in which some human rights are supported by appeal to needs and some by appeal to other human interests such as the interest in autonomy (Tasioulas 2002, 2009–2010).

I shall attempt to address each of these three obstacles in turn.[5] But first let me indicate why needs appear, at least prima facie, to provide suitable justificatory grounds for human rights. One reason is that when we identify something as a human need, we identify it as an essential element in human life, and this gives it the right kind of moral urgency to support human rights. Infringing human rights is meant to be a serious matter: protecting them may be costly. If we begin with human interests in general, we draw no line between relatively weighty and relatively trivial interests, but it does not seem that the latter could ground human rights. We have to discriminate among interests, and by appealing to needs we single out those that have the greatest moral weight. A second reason is that human needs are choice-insensitive. People can of course choose to act in such a way that their needs go unfulfilled – they can refuse the food that is offered them, for example – but they cannot choose whether to have the needs in the first place. This again matches the justificatory requirement for human rights, which are supposed to be independent of the particular ways in which people choose to live their lives.

At this point, however, we confront the first objection to human needs as a ground for human rights, which is that needs do not in fact have the objective status that I have just been taking for granted. Even if at the individual level needs are choice-insensitive, once we move to the social level they are not. Needs, it seems, are always socially defined. What a person needs depends upon the society in which she lives, and the conditions that prevail there. So talk of human needs is in one important way misleading. We do not have needs simply as human beings, but always as socially embedded human beings. Human rights, on the other hand, must be universal in scope: the list we come up with must be the same for people everywhere.

There are two main versions of this objection. The first focuses attention on the way in which needs appear to depend on a society's level of development; the richer the society, the more extensive the needs of its citizens.[6] Even if we can speak of people having basic needs for housing, education or healthcare, we cannot say what level of provision of these goods is sufficient to meet their needs. What is conventionally considered to be a minimum acceptable level for people living in the developed West is far higher than for people living in Sub-Saharan Africa, say. A possible response to this is that although the list of human rights is universal, the actual level of provision required to fulfil each right is socially relative. But this is surely not satisfactory, and it would have the paradoxical consequence that human rights might in some circumstances impose obligations on people in poor societies to meet the expanded needs of people in richer societies.

A better response to the first objection, in my view, is to draw a distinction between human needs proper and what I will call *societal* needs.[7] Societal needs are the needs people have qua members of particular societies, and they can be defined as the conditions that must be fulfilled in order for a person to lead a minimally decent life in the society to which he or she belongs. Such needs depend on contingent social norms that define standards of decency; someone whose needs are not met may still be able to function properly in a physical sense, but he will not be able to participate in the full range of activities that are regarded by those around him as together making up an adequate human life (I assume here that there will be broad agreement within the society over what these activities are, and therefore over what counts as a need and what does not). How, then, should human needs be understood? We must look behind the contingent norms that define societal needs to find a core set of activities that together define an adequate human life *as such*. Human needs can then be identified as the conditions necessary for someone to engage in each of the activities that make up this set without having to forgo any of the others.

The question that arises here is whether there is indeed such a generic human form of life over and above the many specific forms of life that human beings have created for themselves. I believe that such an idea lies behind many of the practical judgements that we make, even if we are not fully clear as to where its boundaries lie. For example, we would have little hesitation in judging that those held captive in the Guantanamo Bay detention centre are unable to lead a minimally decent human life while they remain incarcerated. We can make that judgement without knowing anything about the societies from which the inmates came, or about their specific cultural beliefs. How might we respond if challenged to justify this judgement? Leave aside for present purposes the various harms that have been inflicted on the captives in the course of interrogation, since the denial of human needs here requires no underlining, and consider just the impact of being incarcerated in such an institution. To show that the inmates are being denied the opportunity for a minimally decent life, we would point to facts such as these: Guantanamo inmates cannot engage in productive work; they cannot build houses; they cannot form friendships or raise families; they have few opportunities for recreation, and cannot plan the pattern of their days; they cannot participate in religious or other cultural rituals; and so forth. The absence of these opportunities indicates unmet needs that belong to the captives merely as human beings. Individual people may of course be unable to fulfil one of their needs, or may choose not to because of the particular plan of life they have adopted – say if for religious reasons they decide not to raise a family. So it would be too strong to say that a person cannot lead a decent human life unless all of the needs on the list of human needs are satisfied.[8] Nevertheless, if a person lacks the opportunity to meet one of these needs, this threatens her ability to lead a decent life, understood in terms of a core set of activities such as those listed above. To say that X is a human need, therefore, is to say that a person who lacks X cannot lead a decent life unless he chooses not to avail himself of X despite having the opportunity to do so.[9]

The form that these core activities take in any society will naturally depend on the conditions and conventions that prevail in that society. So human needs will present themselves as societal needs, which are likely to be more extensive in the sense of requiring more resources, or more specific resources, to satisfy them. The human need for food takes the form of a need for socially acceptable food – food that does not contravene cultural taboos – in each society. But we can still distinguish the human need as such in these cases. Since it is human needs, not societal needs, that are being invoked to ground human rights, these rights can be understood as universal in form, even though what we must do to fulfil them may in some cases have to take account of social circumstances.[10]

So far I have been trying to meet the objection that holds that needs cannot ground human rights because they are socially relative, in particular by being relative to levels of economic development. But an alternative objection holds that they are *culturally* relative, in the sense of being dependent on culturally specific notions of what is important in human life. An example may illustrate the objection. Suppose someone asks whether religious education is a human need – religious education in the sense of being thoroughly immersed in the beliefs and rituals of a particular religion. It seems that this question cannot be answered without first settling the question of the proper place of religion in human life. Suppose one holds that religious faith and practice are of supreme importance. Then it would seem that a minimally decent life must include these, and someone who is not given the kind of education that would allow her to lead such a life has one of her essential needs left unfulfilled. From this perspective, the fact that many people in the contemporary world appear to live lives that are more than minimally decent despite having little or no religious content cuts no ice; a minimally decent life must, inter alia, be a religious life. Moreover from the same perspective it may well appear that needs that are assumed by others to count as basic human needs, such as the need for sexual relationships, should be deleted from the list.

The thrust of this objection is that the only human needs that are capable of being defended cross-culturally will be basic physiological needs, such as needs for food and water; and there is no guarantee that even these will be given priority over other needs whose urgency springs from culturally specific notions of value. Clearly, this would provide too slender a basis for an adequate theory of human rights. So we must find some way to deflect the force of the cultural objection. I want to say two things in response to it.

The first is that we may be able to salvage the idea of an agreed set of human needs by formulating these in a suitably abstract way. We may not agree that there is a need for religious education as such, but we can agree that there is a need for education, and this can be spelt out as a need for an education that prepares children to take part in the range of activities that together constitute a decent life in the society to which they belong. So the specific content of the need will depend upon the character of the society in question, and in the case of a society in which religious participation is a central activity this will obviously mean that education must have a significant religious component. It is true of course that this way of understanding the need will not satisfy the person who stands within the culture we are considering. From his perspective there is a primitive human need for religious education, not simply a derivative need that arises in a society in which religion plays an important role in structuring social life. Such a person must think that children in Western liberal societies who receive an essentially secular education are not having one of their human needs met. On the other hand, it would be difficult for him to deny that the education that is provided is necessary for children who as a matter of fact are going to live in these societies, and must therefore be equipped with certain skills if they are going to participate fully in economic and social life. He must admit, in other words, that when children in Western societies are taught to be literate and numerate, their human need for education is being met – albeit, from his perspective, not in full. So the position is that we have cross-cultural agreement on there being a human need for education, and partial, but not complete, agreement on what this means more concretely in given circumstances.

My second response to the problem of cultural relativity is that we may be able to agree on a list of human needs without necessarily agreeing on the relative importance of meeting different needs on the list if for practical reasons it is impossible to fulfil them all. If we define human needs with reference to the core activities that make up the human form of life, there is likely to be disagreement across cultures about how important each of these activities is relative to the others. Some may rank productive work more highly than religious observance; others may reverse this priority. These relative weightings are likely to make a difference when it comes to drawing up a list of human rights, particularly when it is a question of delineating the scope of one right as against that of another. Let me illustrate this point: consider the right to liberty and the right to personal security. The boundaries of these rights are not fixed. In order to protect the right to security, we need to restrict the freedom to act of those threaten it, for example by incarcerating criminals convicted of violent crimes. But where the balance should be struck – for example, in terms of the length of sentences imposed on particular offenders – cannot be determined without weighing the relative importance of the human needs that lie behind the rights in question. This exercise might yield somewhat different results in different societies, and one could not then say that human rights were not being respected because society S imposed greater restrictions on the freedom of those who posed a security threat than we would wish to impose in our society (there may perhaps be a threshold beyond which we would judge that the right to freedom was being infringed). A similar point can be made about the case where, because of a scarcity of resources, human rights to education and to basic healthcare cannot both be fully met together; which should then be given priority will depend on socially specific judgements about the relative importance of the two human needs at stake. It should not be part of a theory of human rights to offer an authoritative resolution in such a case.

Let me try to summarize my argument about the objectivity of human needs. I have said that we should understand them as setting out the conditions for a decent human life, and a person has a decent human life when she or she has the opportunity to engage in a range of human activities that are reiterated across societies in such a way that we can speak meaningfully of a human form of life. It is therefore possible to say of people in a particular society that they fail to recognize need X, because they do not see that without X, people cannot engage in one or more of the core activities. In that sense they have made a mistake about human needs. On the other hand, since these generic activities always take concrete forms, there can legitimately be disagreement about needs that arise in relation to any one such concrete form; in my example there cannot be legitimate disagreement about the human need for education, but there can be disagreement about whether there is a human need for *religious* education specifically. There can also be legitimate disagreement about the relative weight that should be given to different human needs in cases of conflict. In the light of this, my suggestion is that human needs are sufficiently objective to ground human rights; the disagreement that can legitimately arise about them does not undermine the doctrine of human rights once we understand the purpose that that doctrine is meant to serve. It does not attempt to cover all of the needs that should be met, as a matter of justice, in any particular society, but to specify a minimum set of freedoms and resources, in whose absence the legitimacy of the local regime is put in question and global obligations are potentially triggered.

But even if we restrict ourselves to the set of human needs that are *not* subject to reasonable disagreement, there is still the question whether meeting these needs in full may impose requirements that are too demanding from the perspective of human rights. This is the second obstacle that appears to lie in the path leading from human needs to human rights – what I called the problem of overshoot. People, in other words, will need certain things that they cannot claim as human rights, because to allow that claim would be to demand too much of others – of governments in the first place, but through them of the people who would have to supply the resources to satisfy the need. Medical needs provide the most obvious illustration (Weale 2012). Some medical conditions require round-the-clock supervision, for example; others require the supply of scarce body parts. If the human right to medical care were interpreted so as to require that these needs were met, then although a government could take steps to try to ensure this, there is no guarantee that it will succeed unless it is prepared to coerce people into taking on the necessary supervisory roles or giving up their body parts. But this would mean interfering with what seem prima facie to be the human rights of the people being coerced – rights to personal freedom and bodily integrity – which in turn would be justified by *their* human needs. One person's need conflicts with the needs of others in such cases, and it therefore seems impossible to appeal to needs themselves to resolve the conflict and establish where human rights begin and end. If we stipulate that the human right to medical care does *not* include the right to round-the-clock supervision or to be given vital organs, then it seems that we are arbitrarily deciding that one set of needs should count when rights are at stake while another set should not.

Is there any way forward here? The first step is to grasp that we should not see the justificatory relationship between human needs and human rights as one-to-one, in normal cases. Perhaps occasionally there will be a need that is so clear and so compelling that it generates a corresponding right without much argument. But more often a particular need will lend support to several rights, while on the other hand a particular right may be grounded in several distinct needs. For instance the human need for social contact with other human beings can help to ground rights to freedom of movement, freedom of association, and freedom of expression. What this suggests is that we should see the justificatory relationship as holding between the set of human needs and the set of human rights – the justification for the latter being that by recognizing the human rights included in the set, we provide those who hold the rights with the best possible opportunity to have their human needs met. That would mean that where needs conflict – where one person's need for X can only be met by sacrificing other people's need for Y – we have to decide which need takes precedence before we can decide how the corresponding human right should be defined. We cannot at this stage assume anything about human rights themselves – we cannot discount the need for X on the grounds that meeting it would require us to deny others their human right to Y, for we have not yet settled that there *is* a human right to Y, as opposed to some more restricted right.[11]

How then should we proceed? We might begin by considering which need was more significant, asking what would be the impact on someone's life if the need was not satisfied. This would mean, however, always giving priority to medical need in the kind of case I am considering. If John is suffering from kidney failure and is not provided with a transplanted kidney, then he will either die, or at least will have to undergo the rigours of a dialysis regime with its attendant side-effects. If Frank is forced to supply a kidney to John against his will, he may find this a traumatic experience and suffer the psychological after-effects, but the risk that he will subsequently suffer a loss of bodily functioning is very small, and so he is much more likely to be able to lead a sufficiently good life than John will be if the kidney is not transplanted. So following this line of thought, in place of a general right to bodily integrity which would prohibit any taking or use of a person's body parts without her consent, we would have a more limited right that allowed the compulsory taking of organs in circumstances where the predicted cost to the supplier was much smaller than the predicted cost to the recipient if the body part is not transferred.

Most of us would find this conclusion repugnant, but are we right to do so? The argument I have just sketched in favour of limiting the right to bodily integrity focused on just a single need, the need to have functioning bodily organs. But if we think about why we value the full-blown right to bodily integrity, there is clearly more to it than that. Having control over our bodies, and in particular being protected against unwanted interference by others, is important to our sense of ourselves as human agents in a number of respects. Why, for example, do people find it distressing and unsettling to be touched in unwanted ways by others even though no physical harm is involved? Or why would I feel violated if, for example, somebody came in and spray-painted my body while I was asleep (with no harmful side-effects)? What is wrong with forcing somebody to use their body in a way that goes against their will, again in the absence of any further physical harm? This suggests that there are a number of human needs related to the body that together go to justify the right of bodily integrity of which the need to have a functioning set of vital organs is only one. We cannot just look at John and Frank and ask whose need is more urgent, and therefore who should be granted the corresponding right. Instead we have to ask about the overall impact, in terms of fulfilling needs, of having an unqualified right of bodily integrity against having a more qualified one. Indeed we have eventually to go further, because each of these rights will have to be integrated into the full set of human rights. That will mean considering, among other things, how one right might either support or hinder the fulfilment of other rights. In the present case, for example, a right to bodily integrity supports the right to freedom of conscience, since it disallows a person being compelled to let her body to be used in ways that contravene her beliefs (many Jehovah's Witnesses, for instance, reject organ transplants as part of their wider rejection of blood transfusions which they see as contrary to biblical teaching).[12]

The approach I have suggested may also help to address the problem of needs that clearly cannot be translated directly into human rights, such as needs for love and friendship. Although there is no way to guarantee the satisfaction of these needs by legal or political means, by creating a structure of human rights we can also help to create an environment in which a person's chances to fulfil these needs are maximized. As suggested above, rights such as freedom of movement and association make it easier for people to satisfy their need for social contact, and a fortiori for these deeper emotional needs. Thus such needs can support human rights, while also giving individual people reasons for action that go well beyond anything that could be turned into a formal obligation.

That concludes my response to the problem of overshoot. It is clear that the moral force of needs carries us well beyond human rights, but that does not constitute an obstacle to giving needs a foundational role in debates about rights, provided their role is understood in the way I have suggested – that is holistically rather than in terms of one-to-one connections. This also allows me to restate slightly the conclusion of my earlier argument about cultural relativity. I suggested that the way particular rights were defined would depend upon the relative importance that a culture attaches to different human needs. We can now see that this suggestion should really apply to the *set* of human rights, taking into account the role a particular right will have in supporting other rights as well as its direct function in fulfilling specific needs. For each society, then, it will be possible to say which set of human rights, more precisely defined, best meets its members' needs. This does not mean that it will be impossible for people from different societies to agree upon formal declarations of rights. It just means that when these documents are being put to use, for example to criticize government policy or to mount a legal challenge, there has to be what European lawyers call a 'margin of appreciation' which permits some flexibility in the way the documents are interpreted in different states.[13]

Let me turn finally to the problem of undershoot. Are needs a rich enough source of human rights – can they generate all of the human rights that we think should belong on the canonical list, or do we have to supplement them with other values, in other words embrace some version of pluralism in our justificatory theory of human rights?

The main concern here is that an appeal to human needs may be able to explain and justify what we might call *material* human rights, such as rights to subsistence and basic healthcare, but it is much less clear that it can explain liberties, like the right of free speech, or political rights, such as rights to vote or form political associations. It does not look at first glance as though there are human needs that will go unmet if these latter rights are not recognized; it does not, in other words, seem that our idea of a minimally decent human life must include the activities these rights protect as necessary components. So it seems that either we will have to broaden the grounds that we appeal to in support of human rights, or else we will have to shorten the list of human rights significantly, leaving out some of the rights that feature prominently in familiar documents such as the United Nations Declaration.

I want to defend some shortening of the list, and not merely by cutting out rights such as the notorious right to periodic holidays with pay that somehow found its way into the UN Declaration. If we understand the purpose of a human rights doctrine, as I suggested earlier, to be one of specifying the minimum entitlements that people everywhere can claim as a matter of justice, first from their own governments and failing that from the wider international community, then we must at the same time acknowledge that the formal documents in which human rights are codified, including the UN Declaration, often go beyond this purpose. They do not merely specify a minimum, but set out aspirations that states should try to meet in favourable circumstances. Indeed this purpose is hinted at at the beginning of the Declaration, when it is described as setting a 'common standard of achievement' for all peoples, who are urged to 'strive by teaching and education to promote respect for these rights and freedoms, and by progressive measures, national and international, to secure their universal and effective recognition and observance' (Brownlie and Goodwin-Gill 2006, p. 24). There is nothing wrong with aiming high and setting out a long-term goal to be achieved by 'progressive measures', but this is different from listing rights whose fulfilment is a matter of justice here and now.

Therefore, the issue is not whether a needs approach can deliver all of the rights found in the UN Declaration, or any of the later documents drawn up in its wake, but whether it can produce a catalogue that is long enough and full enough to represent the minimum demands of global justice. Let me suggest three ways in which we can justify civil and political rights on the basis of human needs.

First, a number of such rights will follow directly from the idea of the conditions that are necessary for a minimally decent human life. Rights against slavery, against torture, against arbitrary arrest or detention, all fall into this category. Human beings need to be protected against these forms of oppression if they are going to be able to plan and organize their lives securely. Freedom of conscience and expression, and freedom of association, can be justified in the same way, once we recognize that a minimally decent life must involve having the opportunity to communicate and interact with others. The fact that a small number of human beings have chosen at certain moments to withdraw from society and live as hermits should not obscure the equally obvious fact that the human form of life itself is social and made up of shared practices. For a person to have a minimally decent life, she must have the opportunity to engage in these common practices are far as she is able, and for that she needs to be able to associate with others, speak, sing, dance, etc., depending on the case. Rights that protect such elementary freedoms can in this way be justified by appeal to the rudimentary needs of a social animal.

Second, among the needs that human beings have is the need for recognition. This is a difficult idea, and one should resist the temptation to try to extract too much from it. It seems clear, however, that humans cannot lead minimally decent lives unless they achieve a certain standing, at least in the eyes of those who matter to them. Being systematically demeaned, ignored, treated as a non-person, undermines a person's capacity to lead a decent life even if the material conditions for such a life are present and the freedom to lead it is secured. So this may justify rights to be given a certain legal status and to be protected against certain forms of arbitrary treatment. The UN Declaration states that 'everyone has the right to recognition everywhere as a person before the law' (Article 6) and also that 'everyone has the right to an effective remedy ... for acts violating the fundamental rights granted him by the constitution or by law' (Article 8) (Brownlie and Goodwin-Gill 2006, p. 25). These formulations are somewhat vague, but I think they capture the idea I am invoking here. Recognition in this narrow legal sense is a necessary, although perhaps not sufficient, condition for being recognized as a person in a wider social sense. Sandwiched in between these two rights is the right to 'equal protection against any discrimination'. Here I think we have to tread more carefully. It does not seem that a general right against discrimination, in the sense of a right against the existence of any law or policy that treats different categories of people differently, could be justified on the basis of the human need for recognition. That need can be met by being recognized as a person who belongs to a certain category or occupies a certain role. So a society that enshrined clear distinctions of status, but nevertheless provided secure recognition for people qua members of each status group, could not be faulted from this perspective. Liberals would of course criticize such an arrangement in the name of equality, but a strong, universal, right of non-discrimination has to be seen as an expression of this liberal world-view, and therefore not a human right according to the theory I am advocating.

Third, some civil and political rights can be justified instrumentally, on the grounds that they are necessary to protect other rights whose basis in human needs has already been established. The right to a fair trial and the right to political representation fall into this category. One could not argue that these rights correspond directly to human needs. But it has long been recognized that a person who lacks such rights is vulnerable to having other, more basic, rights violated or taken away entirely. Core freedoms such as freedom of expression are only secure if there are legal procedures in place to protect people who might otherwise be subject to arbitrary interference by agents of the state. Equally, material rights such as the right to subsistence have to be protected by forms of representation, democratic or otherwise, that put pressure on state officials to ensure that the right is fulfilled. Rights such as these are often regarded as intrinsically valuable, and in liberal societies they have an important expressive function as component parts of the idea of equal citizenship. But if we are going to justify them by appeal to human needs that are universal in scope, then the justification we offer has to be instrumental, involving an appeal to the accumulated weight of evidence that where these civil and political rights are not implemented, other rights are very likely to be violated.[14]

It might be argued here that in order to deal with the problem of undershoot, I have tacitly adopted a pluralistic grounding for human rights, referring to different human interests to justify different rights rather than grounding them all in human needs. For example, I have appealed to a need for recognition, but could one drop the reference to need and simply say that it matters greatly to human beings that they are given a certain kind of recognition, and it is this interest that explains why there is a human right to legal status and to legal remedy for breaches of rights? Now it is certainly true that the account I have given appeals to a wide range of human needs, not merely to the physical necessities of life, but it is not just a verbal manoeuvre to describe them all as needs. The key distinction, as I see it, is between conditions that are simply of great value to human beings, and conditions in the absence of which they cannot lead decent lives. In drawing this distinction, I am not tacitly assuming value pluralism. It may be true that what human beings value most differs greatly. But suppose, for instance, that every human being took great pleasure in listening to opera – suppose it really mattered to them to go to the opera from time to time. It would still not be the case that opera attendance was a human need. People's lives would be a bit colourless if it was no longer possible to go to the opera, they would sigh wistfully when they remembered the days when they could, but still they could lead decent lives without that wonderful experience. Even a universally shared interest, I am suggesting, cannot ground a human right, whereas a universal need can. Why is this so? Rights give rise to obligations: human rights create obligations on governments and others to protect and fulfil them. No such obligations arise when values and interests that are not needs are at stake. Certainly if there were a universally shared interest in opera, there would be a good reason to promote it. A Bill Gates or George Soros who offered massive opera subsidies would be a great benefactor of humanity in the circumstances I am imagining. But there could not be an obligation to do this, on anyone's part. I cannot explain why needs can ground obligations whereas other interests, however strong, do not; that is a fundamental intuition that I take for granted here. But if the intuition is correct, then for human rights to be genuine, obligation-imposing rights, they must be justified by reference to human needs. So it is incumbent on us to show that all the needs we appeal to in the grounding process really are needs. If that is not the case – if the justification for human rights is in fact pluralistic – then the doctrine acquires a different status. It becomes something like a statement of human priorities – these are the freedoms and resources that we value most. That might be worth having, if it were possible to obtain agreement on its content, but it would not serve the purpose that I have suggested the doctrine of human rights is intended to serve.

Therefore, to summarize, I have identified three obstacles to grounding human rights on human needs. The first is the problem of objectivity – are human needs sufficiently objective to play this foundational role? In response to this I distinguished human needs proper from what I called societal needs, and suggested that although there was still some scope for legitimate disagreement about how human needs should be concretely specified, this was not so wide as to undermine their objective status. The second is the problem of overshoot. In response to this, I suggested that the grounding relationship should be seen as holding between the set of human needs and the set of human rights, so that where needs conflict, we make trade-offs before specifying the optimum set of rights. The third is the problem of undershoot. Here I suggested three ways in which human needs can ground civil and political rights – directly, in some cases, instrumentally in others, and specifically through the need for recognition, in yet others. And I have suggested that this can be done without venturing down the primrose path of pluralism.

Having spelt out my favoured method of grounding human rights, I want finally to return to Peter Jones and his formulation of the challenge posed by cultural diversity for human rights. In responding to that challenge, his main concern is with the question whether human rights can be seen as a threat to non-Western cultures. Is the doctrine of human rights an individualistic doctrine in a sense that sets it at odds with cultures that place a great deal of value on communal activities of various kinds? I think that Jones's strategy here is very successful. He distinguishes different senses in which we might describe human rights doctrine as individualistic, and then points out that once the relevant sense is identified we can see that human rights pose no necessary threat to communal cultures; indeed they may help to protect the conditions under which such cultures can flourish and develop as their members exercise rights of cultural self-determination (Jones 2000b, esp. pp. 203–204, 208–211; 2000a, pp. 42–45). Thereby he gives us an argument that shows why non-Western cultures should not *reject* human rights as a threat to their way of life. However this is not quite the same as an argument for why, positively, they should embrace them. As I suggested earlier, Jones in his later writings effectively presents human rights as a recipe for cultural toleration: these are the rights that will allow each person, or each group of people, to live according to their own ideas of what is valuable in life. But if that is going to be the selling point, then why not move directly to a doctrine of cultural non-interference: why not say that each culture simply has the right to organize its members' lives according to their own standards of value without interference from others? Human rights doctrine does not go so far, because it *does* justify interference in cases where a politically organized culture restricts freedoms or denies opportunities in a way that infringes its members' basic rights. In Jones' own words, it is 'a fighting doctrine' (Jones 1996, p. 183; 2000a, p. 28): it fights against rights abuses whether or not they have a cultural defence. ('Fighting' here should not of course be taken literally: what form the action to protect human rights should take will depend upon the case.)

But if that is so, and if we want to be able to justify human rights to people living in different cultures even in cases where we are going to appeal to these rights to condemn some of their practices and encourage or possibly require change, then we require foundations. We must be able to explain why there is a right to bodily integrity that prohibits compulsory female circumcision, or a right to freedom of conscience that prohibits people being required to participate in their country's official religion. My suggestion has been that a theory of human needs can do this. It is nonpartisan by virtue of the fact that it rests upon the idea of a minimally decent human life that everyone should accept simply because they themselves participate in one or other version of the human form of life and can therefore recognize its essential components. It is also an advantage of the human needs approach that the list of rights it produces is not too ambitious. It does not, for example, generate a right to full-blown democracy or to unlimited freedom of religious practice. The list may therefore disappoint Western liberals who want it to play a standard-setting role and to use it to criticize their own governments for various lapses. But equally it becomes a more powerful weapon when turned against regimes that really do make it impossible for their subjects to live lives that anyone could regard as minimally decent.

Acknowledgements

An earlier version of this paper was written for the conference entitled 'The Value and Limits of Rights: A Conference in Honour of Peter Jones', Newcastle University, Newcastle upon Tyne, UK, 25–26 February 2010; parts of it were also presented to a conference on 'Needs and Values', University of Basel, Basel, Switzerland, 17–18 September 2010. The author is grateful to both audiences for their comments and suggestions, and especially to Barbara Schmitz and Rowan Cruft for their help in preparing this revised version of the text.

Notes

1. Deciding how this responsibility should be distributed among those who might bear it, and how demanding are the ensuing obligations, are separate (and difficult) issues. I have discussed them in Miller (2001, 2007, chs 4, 9; 2009).

2. For my own critique, see Miller (2007, pp. 174–178). See also the critique of Rawls on human rights in Jones (1996).
3. See also the following passage:
   It may be that different rights have different foundations. If we recognize many sorts of value and if we do not accept that those many sorts of value can be reduced to a single value, it may be that different sorts of rights stem from different sorts of value. After all, rights to life, to freedom of expression, to a fair trial and to social security are rights to very different things. If people have rights to all of those very different sorts of things, they may have them for very different sorts of reason. (Jones 1994, p. 118).
4. For another defence of pluralism, see Tasioulas (2002).
5. I draw in what follows on my discussion in Miller (2007, ch. 7), while trying at various points to address weaknesses in that discussion.
6. This objection is pursued in Jones (1996, ch. 7).
7. For this distinction and a fuller discussion of the relationship between human needs and societal needs, see Schmitz (n.d.).
8. Alert readers may at this point wonder whether it would not be better to ground human rights on *capabilities* rather than on needs, since the capabilities approach, whose two most influential defenders are Martha Nussbaum and Amartya Sen, emphasizes the distinction between capabilities and functionings: a capability is an opportunity to achieve a functioning that need not be taken up if the person who has the capability chooses otherwise. For the application of this approach to human rights, see Nussbaum (1997) and Sen (2004). It is often said that a needs approach overlooks this distinction and can lead to paternalistic policies where people are obliged to have what they need whether they like it or not. As the above text shows, however, this by no means follows. One can first define human needs and then say that what matters practically is that each person should have the *opportunity* to satisfy their needs so defined.
9. This definition needs to be refined to deal with the problem of people who lack the capacity to engage in one of the core activities I have identified – say people with severe physical disabilities that limit the extent of their bodily movement. We do not want to say that they cannot have a decent life. Equally, however, we do want to say that sufficient freedom of movement is in other cases essential to such a life – so there is a human need for freedom of movement.
10. One can draw the distinction between human needs and societal needs without assuming anything about the relative moral urgency of meeting the two kinds of needs. For an argument that we should not treat basic human needs as more morally demanding than needs that arise within specific forms of social life, see Reader (2007, ch. 5). By implication this means that by grounding human rights on human needs, one does not yet say anything about the relative importance of protecting these rights as against rights of other kinds.
11. My discussion in Miller (2007, pp. 187–188) is vulnerable to this criticism, effectively pressed by Cruft (2010). What follows is an attempt to restate my position in a way that avoids Cruft's critique. Cruft argues that the 'holistic' strategy for moving from needs to rights, while it can avoid begging the question by already taking certain human rights for granted, will nonetheless generate stronger assistance rights (and correspondingly weaker rights to non-interference with the person) than we can accept. I try to show why this does not follow.

12. Of course it would be possible to combine a weaker right to bodily integrity – say one that permitted the state to require people to donate blood or other body parts under certain circumstances – with a right of conscientious refusal that recognized religious grounds for refusing to donate. That would still be a lesser right to freedom of conscience, however, because the onus would be on the person concerned to demonstrate that he or she had such grounds.
13. This is the phrase used by the European Court of Human Rights when it defers to national courts over the interpretation of some element of the European Convention on Human Rights. There may, however, be some ambiguity over its meaning, as suggested by Letsas (2006).
14. An obvious example here would be Sen's (1999, chs 6–7) research on the (negative) relationship between democracy and famines. In short, 'no substantial famine has ever occurred in any independent country with a democratic form of government and a relatively free press' (p. 152).

References

Brownlie, I. and Goodwin-Gill, G., eds., 2006. *Basic documents on human rights.* 5th edition. Oxford: Oxford University Press.
Cruft, R., 2010. Kamm and Miller on rights' compatibility. *Ethical Theory and Moral Practice*, 13, 393–401.
Jones, P., 1994. *Rights.* Basingstoke: Macmillan.
Jones, P., 1996. International human rights: philosophical or political? *In*: S. Caney, D. George, and P. Jones, eds. *National rights, international obligations.* Boulder, CO: Westview, 183–204.
Jones, P., 1999. Human rights, group rights, and peoples' rights. *Human Rights Quarterly*, 21, 80–107.
Jones, P., 2000a. Human rights and diverse cultures: continuity or discontinuity? *Critical Review of International Social and Political Philosophy*, 3, 27–50.
Jones, P., 2000b. Individuals, communities and human rights. *Review of International Studies*, 26, 199–215.
Letsas, G., 2006. Two concepts of the margin of appreciation. *Oxford Journal of Legal Studies*, 26, 705–732.
Miller, D., 2001. Distributing responsibilities. *Journal of Political Philosophy*, 9, 453–471; repr. in Kuper, A. ed., 2005. *Global responsibilities: who must deliver on human rights?* New York, NY: Routledge, 95–115.
Miller, D., 2007. *National responsibility and global justice.* Oxford: Oxford University Press.
Miller, D., 2009. The responsibility to protect human rights. *In*: L. Meyer, ed. *Legitimacy, justice and public international law.* Cambridge: Cambridge University Press, 232–251.
Nussbaum, M., 1997. Capabilities and human rights. *Fordham Law Review*, 66, 273–300.
Reader, S., 2007. *Needs and moral necessity.* London: Routledge.
Schmitz, B., n.d. How to derive rights from needs. Unpublished.
Sen, A., 1999. *Development as freedom.* Oxford: Oxford University Press.
Sen, A., 2004. Elements of a theory of human rights. *Philosophy and Public Affairs*, 32, 315–356.
Tasioulas, J., 2002. Human rights, universality and the values of personhood: retracing Griffin's steps. *European Journal of Philosophy*, 10, 79–100.
Tasioulas, J., 2009–2010. Taking rights out of human rights. *Ethics*, 120, 647–678.
Weale, A., 2012. The right to health versus good medical care? *Critical Review of International Social and Political Philosophy*, 15 (4), 473–493.

Why liberals should not worry about subsidizing opera

John Horton

School of Politics, International Relations and the Environment, Keele University, Keele, UK

> Peter Jones has consistently defended the position that liberalism must maintain the distinction between the right and the good if it is to be qualitatively different from alternative political theories, and thus resist the charge that liberals are just like any other political theorists in wanting to impose their views on others. In this paper, I not only add my voice to the many who have already challenged the viability of that distinction, but also additionally argue that it is both unnecessary and undesirable to hold that so much of importance hangs on whether or not it can be sustained. I suggest that the dichotomy between neutralist or impartialist liberalism, on the one hand, and what Jones characterizes as the desire 'merely to impose a favoured form of life upon others', on the other hand, is too sharp, and hence at best misleading and at worst mistaken. This is because, or so I argue, not all forms of favouring some values or ideals over others can plausibly be presented as the imposition of a favoured form of life. Rather, we risk trivializing what is objectionable about imposing a particular form of life on people against their will if we treat every departure from strict liberal neutrality as necessarily instances of such an illiberal imposition.

Introduction

> There are also many others (myself included) who still hope that something approximating to the neutralist position can be sustained for, if liberals have ultimately to accept that they, no less than their opponents, seek merely to impose a favoured form of life upon others, liberalism will have lost much of its distinctiveness and appeal. (Jones 1989, p. 34)

The above quotation neatly encapsulates the view that I here want to call into question. It comes from an article by Peter Jones, now over 20 years old, but it expresses a sentiment to which, if anything, he seems subsequently to have continued to be at least as firmly attached. In that article, in the course of a characteristically perceptive and fair-minded discussion of the idea of a neutral state, and immediately preceding the quote, he nonetheless concedes that there does 'seem to be a real difficulty in maintaining the sharp distinction between the right and the good that the neutralist position requires' (Jones 1989, p. 33).[1] However, notwithstanding any such difficulty, it is taken by Jones to be a matter of real importance for liberalism that it should be able to maintain the distinction between the right and the good, for it is this that effectively underpins 'neutralist' or 'impartialist' liberalism, and in so doing distinguishes liberalism as a qualitatively different kind of view to that of its 'opponents'. By contrast, I want not only to add my voice to the many who have already challenged the viability of that distinction, but also to claim that it is both unnecessary and undesirable to hold that so much hangs on whether or not it can be sustained. In this regard, I shall suggest that the implicit dichotomy between the neutralist or impartialist position, on the one hand, and, on the other hand, what Jones characterizes as the desire 'merely to impose a favoured form of life upon others' is at best misleading, and at worst simply mistaken. This is because, or so I shall argue, not all forms of favouring some values or ideals over others can plausibly be presented as the *imposition* of a favoured form of life. Rather, I want to suggest that we risk trivializing what *is* objectionable about the imposition of a form of life on people against their will if we treat every departure from strict liberal neutrality as an instance of such an imposition of a favoured form of life.

These reflections on what I regard as a misguidedly demanding approach towards what, from any defensible liberal point of view, should be regarded as essentially innocuous outcomes of legitimate democratic political processes are prompted in part by the fact that even a liberal as sensitive, sophisticated and relatively undoctrinaire as Jones should interpret the supposed ideal of liberal neutrality as strictly as he does. That he does so can be vividly captured by a comment that he once made in public discussion: this is that 'the real test of a liberal is whether one believes that it is permissible for the state to subsidise opera'.[2] Of course, the comment need not have been specifically about opera; for it is but an example of a familiar claim about what liberalism supposedly requires if it is to respond appropriately to the fact that people have different conceptions of what is valuable or worth pursuing, differing conceptions of how people should live their lives, which cannot be shown beyond reasonable doubt to be either right or wrong.[3] And, although some liberals claim to have found the antecedents of such a view at least as far back as John Locke, the full-blown theory of liberal neutrality appears to be a relatively recent development in the history of liberal thinking, perhaps beginning with John Rawls's theory of justice, although the term neutrality does not figure at all in *A Theory of Justice* (1999) and impartiality does so only in the context of the Utilitarian idea of the impartial spectator, which Rawls of course rejects. There is, I believe, a potentially extraordinarily interesting history or genealogy of liberal theory waiting to be written in which the trajectory of its development in the last third of the twentieth century is charted and explained.

However, that is not a task to which I intend to contribute, not least because I am not competent to do so. Instead, my aim is to explore what Jones's comment about subsidizing opera reveals about the limits of this kind of liberalism and what underpins it: in doing so I seek to show that this is not the best way to think about liberalism. It is not so much a matter of presenting some knock-down argument against such a view, but of seeking to undercut and unsettle some of the assumptions and arguments that inform it; of avoiding becoming fixated on a particular theory, however seductive it may it appear, rather than focusing on what is truly important about liberalism. And, it should perhaps be added, I do so from a position that is sympathetic to the liberal cause, broadly understood. Indeed, one possible way of thinking about the exercise that follows is that it represents an attempt to defend the *spirit* of liberalism from a certain kind of liberal *theorist*.

I

A more thorough and rigorous discussion than that offered here would need to give closer attention to the clarification of key ideas and to mapping more carefully the landscape of liberal theory. As I have already indicated, however, the kind of liberalism on which I shall focus typically has 'neutrality' or 'impartiality' at its heart (although it should be noted that these terms can have different imports in different contexts).[4] It is also associated with the view that now gets labelled 'political liberalism', although not all political liberals would endorse it. Indeed, for reasons that will be explained shortly, it is not at all clear (to me at least) whether Rawls himself, who is usually thought of as the leading exponent of political liberalism, consistently embraces it. I believe, though, that Jones, along with many others, does.[5] Although he has not set out in any comprehensive and systematic way his theory of liberalism (which is surely our loss), there does appear to be a reasonably settled vision of liberalism that informs his work, and that can be discerned without too much difficulty, especially in a number of his writings on toleration, recognition and the problems of dealing with moral and cultural diversity (Jones 1998, 2003, 2006a, 2006b, 2007).

It is in his generally excellent discussion of how best to address cultural diversity that Jones brings out most explicitly why he believes that the neutralist or impartialist strategy is the appropriate one to adopt. In a key passage, which will be central to my subsequent argument, he begins by explaining what he means by a neutralist or impartial strategy for accommodating cultural diversity:

> By a 'neutral' or 'impartial' strategy, I mean one that is first not drawn from any particular culture; second, that does not seek to privilege any particular culture; and third, that, as far as possible allows or enables people to live according to their own cultures and refrains from imposing alternative modes of life upon them. The last of these three elements of impartiality is necessary if we are to show concern and respect for people's cultural identities, and the first two are required if we are to show that concern and respect equally. (Jones 1998, p. 38)

Neutrality or impartiality is not, for Jones and other such liberals, to be assessed in terms of the consequences or effects of a law or policy, but in terms of its justification: it is the reasoning for the policy or law that must be appropriately neutral in neither drawing upon nor intentionally privileging the values or practices of any particular culture. In seeking such a justification, he writes, 'we have to climb out of the perspective of any particular culture and address the world of cultures, as it were "from the outside"' (Jones 1998, p. 33). That is: the neutralist approach is about adopting a perspective that is in some significant respect external to any particular culture, and which justifies state action in terms that are not based on and do not aim to favour or promote the values or ideals of any one culture in preference to any other. This is quite compatible with the results of a policy that is neutrally justified in fact impacting differentially on various cultures. Not only will this often be unavoidable, but crucially it does not of itself impugn the validity of the claim that a law or policy is, in the relevant sense, neutral or impartial. Whether the latter claim is true in any particular case depends upon how the policy can be justified, not on its consequences.

Should there be any doubt that Jones is himself actually endorsing this neutralist or impartialist approach (and he does not distinguish them) then the following passage should make the point clear:

> Taking cultural diversity seriously *requires* [added emphasis] that we respond to it fairly or justly and that, in turn, requires an approach that is impartial (or neutral) amongst cultures. Claims of impartiality have often been thought peculiarly implausible when applied to cultural diversity, but an impartialist approach is in fact peculiarly appropriate to that form of diversity.
> (Jones 1998, p. 28)

Or, as he expresses the point a little later: 'I shall argue that taking cultural diversity seriously *entails* [my emphasis] providing for it fairly, and that providing for it fairly requires an impartial or neutral approach' (Jones 1998, p. 28). The fair treatment of cultural differences, therefore, involves adopting the external perspective to justify state action. Moreover, it is important to observe the strength of what is being claimed, for this is something to which I will return below: taking cultural diversity seriously *entails* fairness, and fairness *requires* impartiality or neutrality. These are demanding and apparently uncompromising claims.

However, to fully understand Jones's view, we need also to note two further points. The first may seem slightly puzzling, and occurs at the end of a section concerned with reasons as to why we might not always want to pursue impartiality, most of which Jones seems willing to accept. For, as he there writes: 'I myself have no ambition to construct an all-things-considered case for unqualified cultural impartiality' (Jones 1998, p. 52). Why should this be regarded as slightly puzzling? After all, it is surely no more than a realistic and sensible recognition that there are other goods with which cultural impartiality sometimes competes, and in which competition it may not always override those other goods? The reason is that if we agree with the idea that the right is prior to the good, and that cultural impartiality is a matter of the right (that is a matter of justice), both of which Jones appears to endorse, then, unless these countervailing considerations are themselves matters of justice, and it is far from obvious that all those that he mentions could properly be so construed (for example, those labelled 'pragmatic'), it would seem that cultural impartiality should have priority over any non-justice based countervailing considerations. On the other hand, if we were to take cultural impartiality as itself but one conception of the good, Jones's argument would obviously collapse into just the kind of doctrine that neutralist liberalism is not supposed to be. There is good reason, therefore, to believe that this latter is certainly not Jones's view. To be clear, I am entirely sympathetic to an approach that does not fetishize the distinction between the right and the good, and would therefore enthusiastically support the contention that cultural impartiality is only one reason, if a powerful one, among many others for why we might order society one way rather than another. My point, however, is that it is not at all obvious that Jones's kind of impartialist liberal can in consistency be quite so relaxed about this matter.

The second point, which in a way follows on the previous one, is that there is, of course, more than one way of interpreting and arguing for the impartialist/neutralist approach, and there is much lively and interesting internal debate between its proponents as to exactly what form it should take. Somewhat cavalierly, I shall ignore much of this debate, although I will not be able to do so entirely, for reasons to be explained in a moment. What I want to focus on, though, is the essential logic of the argument contained in the first quotation in the preceding paragraph. For, I believe that with characteristic incisiveness Jones pretty much lays bare the line of thought that underlies most, if not perhaps all, forms of neutralist liberalism. In that passage, Jones can be seen to make three claims that can be regarded as integral to a neutralist strategy. These are:

(1) The strategy must not be drawn from any particular culture.
(2) It must not seek to privilege any particular culture.
(3) So far as possible it allows people to live according to their own cultures and refrains from imposing alternative modes of life upon them.

These claims are what fairness or justice, according to the liberal neutralist, requires in the treatment of different cultures, or more properly, as he says, the treatment of the members of different cultures. This approach is, as noted earlier, 'clearly inspired by a distinction between the right and the good' (Jones 1998, p. 38), according to which principles of justice or fair treatment are justified from an appropriate point of view external to any particular culture. And, although he is here specifically discussing cultures, I do not believe that we would do any serious violence to the argument by extending it to those familiar staples of liberal discourse, 'conceptions of the good' or 'comprehensive doctrines' or values more generally.[6] That is how, ultimately, we arrive at the idea that liberalism is incompatible with the state subsidizing opera, if the arguments for doing so depend, for example, upon claims about the intrinsic value of opera. For, that would be to invoke a particular conception of the good in justification of the policy, and the aim of subsidy would be to support that particular conception in preference to some other conceptions.

Before addressing this argument directly, however, it is necessary to acknowledge some of complexities within the broad church of neutralist liberalism that have so far been set aside, and which make for a more confusing picture. First, as Jones notes, impartialist theories can be interpreted in more than one way. Thus, the theories of Chandran Kukathas (Kukathas 2003) and Will Kymlicka (Kymlicka 1989), for instance, lead in very divergent directions when it comes to policy prescriptions, although both claim to be defending a form of neutralist liberalism. Moreover, Brian Barry (Barry 2001), another liberal impartialist, effectively casts a plague on both their houses in a discussion of multiculturalism that is largely dismissive of the views of both of them. I shall return to this question of differing *conceptions* of impartiality, as it might be termed, shortly. At this point, though, I want to draw attention to a second aspect of the complexity of neutralist liberalism. This concerns the strategies that have been adopted for mitigating what can seem, even to some neutralist liberals, to be a less than attractive implication of this view. Not all neutralist liberals are comfortable with the thought that the state may not be permitted to subsidize opera or the arts more generally or to promote other good causes. I shall mention two such strategies, which I label (somewhat non-neutrally in the case of the first) the *special pleading* approach and the *basic structure* approach. The *locus classicus* of the special pleading approach is probably Ronald Dworkin's chapter 'Can a Liberal State Support Art?' (Dworkin

1985, ch. 11). The question in the title is one that he answers in the affirmative, but only so long as the subsidy is to promote diversity and innovation, and does not seek to interfere with the content of art. In this way, Dworkin believes, the state may legitimately subsidize the arts. I should make it clear from the start that I have no real objection to much of what Dworkin claims so far as actual policy is concerned. However, it seems to me, his position is rendered unnecessarily tortuous and considerably less plausible because of his desire to make it consistent with his commitment to liberal neutrality.

Be that as it may, and it is not possible to go into the detail of Dworkin's arguments here, it is true more generally that neutralist liberals may be able to, or at least can certainly try to, defend something like subsidy for opera on grounds consistent with their commitment to the primacy of liberal neutrality. What the special pleading approach does appear to rule out, however, not least in Dworkin's view, is a certain kind of reason for such a subsidy: specifically, any arguments that make some judgement about the worth of the arts. We cannot legitimately claim that the arts should receive state support simply because, for instance, they are good for us or especially valuable. As it is this claim that is of interest here, it should be possible to sidestep such casuistical exercises, as that of Dworkin. For I want to question the conceptual and argumentative structure that means that opera can be subsidized, or other conceptions of the good promoted by the state, only if we can find some neutral justification for doing so; that is, only if there is some reason other than that which almost everyone who believes in subsidizing opera (or any other of the arts) actually thinks *is* the principal reason why it should be subsidized. While Jones must be exempted from the following observation precisely because he eschews such special pleading, it is this tendency that tends to get liberalism a bad name with non-liberals, who are inclined to become highly suspicious when it turns out that liberalism can justify support for those things that liberals typically like, such as the arts, but will deny any resources from the public purse to support, for instance, religious schools or buildings, unless it happens that the latter have already been built and are deemed to be of outstanding architectural interest, in which case the state may be permitted to support them, but only so long as that support has nothing to do with religion!

Let us turn now to the second strategy: the *basic structure* approach. As its name would suggest, this approach has its origins in Rawls. At least in some of his moods, Rawls can be read as arguing that because neutralist arguments are required only to justify the institutions and laws governing the basic structure of society, and because decisions about whether or not to subsidize the arts, for example, would not concern the basic structure (Rawls 1999, pp. 6–10; 1997), whether or not the state should subsidize opera could quite properly be a matter for democratic decision. This interpretation would appear to receive support from a passage such as the following:

> At this point I can only note that public funds for the arts and sciences may be provided through the exchange branch. In this instance there are no restrictions on the reasons citizens may have for imposing upon themselves the requisite taxes. They may assess the merits of these public goods on perfectionist principles. (Rawls 1999, p. 291)

On the other hand, this passage is almost immediately followed by another, which seems to suggest something close to the reverse:

> [T]he principles of justice do not permit subsidising universities and institutes, or opera and the theatre, on the grounds that these institutions are intrinsically valuable. ... Taxation for these purposes can be justified only as promoting directly or indirectly the social conditions that secure the equal liberties and as advancing in an appropriate way the long-term interests of the least advantaged. (Rawls 1999, pp. 291–292)

It is rather hard to see how subsidizing opera would be justifiable on these grounds, and anyway Rawls appears to explicitly exclude the kind of grounds that are of particular interest here – what he calls 'perfectionist' arguments.[7] According to Samuel Freeman, Rawls himself was 'surprised' that some people thought the argument of *A Theory of Justice* committed him to denying that a just democratic society could legitimately subsidize perfectionist social institutions, such as the opera (Freeman 2007, p. 511 n. 15). However, it is this surprise on Rawls's part that is perhaps the more surprising, given some of what he does say about this matter.

Whatever the view of Rawls, however, the neutralism of someone like Barry (1995) does appear to allow for subsidy of opera on just these grounds. Indeed, he goes so far as to say that

> The only possible rationale for subsidization is that there are some artistic endeavours that are of very high quality and need public support either to continue at all or to be accessible to more than a privileged elite. The obvious examples are grand opera, symphonic music and non-commercial theatre. (Barry 2001, p. 198)

Although this is probably not the only plausible rationale for artistic subsidy it is almost certainly the most common, and crucially it is one to which Barry finds no neutralist objection. Within limits of course, on this view, there are some matters on which we can just vote in line with our preferences, whatever people's reasons for voting one way rather than another, and then the state can act according to how the votes stack up. At least some neutralist liberals, therefore, do not think that neutralist justifications are necessary for all aspects of public policy. With regard to them, the argument has to be about the plausibility of how they make such claims consistent with their supposed commitment to neutrality. And it is worries about this that tends to make other neutralist liberals suspicious of views such as those of Barry. Although Jones does not, so far as I can see, directly address this question, it may be possible to infer from what he does say, and not just the informal comment about subsidizing opera, but for instance his remarks about deliberative democracy, that at the very least he would not leave much room for such democratic decision-making in a properly liberal society. However, these complexities make neutralist liberalism a hard target to pin down, and can leave one seemingly quixotically tilting at windmills, or open to accusations of setting up the proverbial straw man; a charge with which anyone who has criticized almost any aspect of liberalism is likely to have become familiar: liberals, rather like erring husbands, are never in the wrong, just misunderstood. However, in so far as some neutralist liberals leave a significant space for public policy decisions supported by 'perfectionist' reasons, then they are largely exempt from the criticisms with which I am specifically concerned here.[8]

As a final preliminary, I should briefly pick up on the reference to 'perfectionist' arguments in the foregoing discussion. In particular, I want to anticipate the claim that I am simply embracing what has become known as perfectionist liberalism, specifically of the kind associated with Joseph Raz. Thus, to be clear, I do not attach primacy to the value of 'autonomy' in the way that Raz (1986, chs 14–15) does. There is, for instance, in my view no reason to believe that people cannot flourish, in the sense of live valuable and meaningful lives, in so-called 'non-autonomy valuing' cultures, even when these cultures operate as minority cultures in societies like our own. And while Raz (1994, ch. 7) seems to have softened his views with regard to such cultures, autonomy continues to have, what could reasonably be described as, a foundational place within his theory. However, not only do I reject the idea that autonomy or any other single value underpins liberalism, rather than a plurality of sometimes competing values, I do not understand liberalism to be committed to promoting *any* particular conception of the good, only that it is not necessarily incompatible with being liberal for a state to do so, subject of course to certain constraints on how it does so.[9] The critique of neutralist liberalism articulated here should not, therefore, be understood as an endorsement of some form of perfectionist liberalism, although it is compatible with certain features of it.

II

So much, then, for these rather lengthy orienting remarks. What, though, is the case against Jones's view? Why should liberals be unconcerned if opera is subsidized by the state from general taxation, including from the taxes of those who attach no value to it, on the grounds that it is a valuable activity worthy of such public support? Little, I have to say in this regard is new, but perhaps there is something distinctive about the way I address Jones's three claims identified earlier, and with the more general contention that justice or fairness in this context necessarily requires neutrality. I begin with Jones's first claim: that the strategy must not be drawn from any particular culture. Here, I make two observations, both of which to some extent draw on and revive arguments made long ago, and in some quarters thought to be *passé*, by so-called 'communitarians', such as Alasdair MacIntyre among others. The first is that it is far from clear that there is much by way of argument available to us that is, if not drawn from a particular culture, at least informed by particular sets of cultural assumptions, broadly understood. I am not here making the point that impartiality might not get much of a hold in the conceptual structure of, for instance, a medieval Samurai warrior. While probably true, fortunately, we do not have to live with medieval Samurai warriors. Arguments may, indeed, be more or less culture specific, and some may be so broad in their specificity that it does not matter politically that we can think of antiquated or imaginary cultures with which they would be incompatible.

However, even a cultural value that is common across all relevant cultures or shared by diverse conceptions of the good, is likely to be subject to differing interpretations and to differing assessments of its importance relative to other goods and values (cf. Miller 2012, Weale 2012). Appeals to a value such as freedom, which may indeed be very widely shared at some level of abstraction, are always appeals to a particular conception of freedom, and always involve some, at least implicit, ranking of its value as against other values. Of course, liberal political theorists are not unaware of this, but one does not have to evince a very high level of scepticism to see that no particular interpretation is demonstrably superior to all others and that any weighting attributed to freedom will in part depend upon the weight that is attached to other values. Moreover, as is often acknowledged, arguments about such matters are commonly rooted in intuitions, which are in turn culturally produced, and also may not be as widely shared as liberals would like to think. In fairness to Jones, though, it will be recalled that the point I am making here is basically the objection that, as mentioned in the opening paragraph above, he agreed represented 'a real difficulty in maintaining the sharp distinction between the right and the good' (Jones 1989, p. 33). While this concession does not lessen the difficulty, given that Jones acknowledges the point, it would be churlish to labour it unduly. However, it is not the only problem.

For instance, this worry also leads to a second, and related, point. It concerns a crucial step in the neutralist argument, and one that is in my view seminal to that argument having any chance of success. Jones (1998) expresses the point as follows:

> The approach I am describing here refrains from ranking cultures in an order of merit and seeks only to provide impartially for people who possess different cultures. The split between the principles that are to regulate cultural diversity and the cultures that they regulate parallels that between the right and the good. Of course, some of what is contained within cultures may more naturally be described as 'principles of right' than as 'conceptions of the good'. But that doesn't matter. We can still distinguish principles contained within diverse cultures from principles designed to provide fairly for diverse cultures. (pp. 38–39)

But how, I want to ask, can this distinction be made at all convincingly? Jones mentions in this context, without committing himself to any one of them, devices such as the original position and the idea of reasonable rejection. But do any of these approaches exist outside of, or as Jones calls it 'external to', a particular culture? Or, in another phrase he uses, how does this 'shift of levels' enable us to see, if not – to borrow a phrase from Thomas Nagel – 'the view from nowhere', at least the view from nowhere in particular? One of the merits of Rawls's account of the construction of the original position is that, at least some of the time, there is no real pretence on his part about how it is built out of a great many cultural assumptions; that is, much of what goes into the veil of ignorance and the rationality of the parties (Rawls 1999, pp. 118–129) and through his use of the method of reflective equilibrium (Rawls 1999, pp. 42–45). And, in *Political Liberalism* (1993), there is explicit acknowledgement that the basic ideas are drawn from and designed for the culture of a 'constitutional democracy' (Rawls 1993, pp. 125–129). It is more complicated to make a similar case with respect to the idea of 'reasonable rejection', but as I have argued elsewhere, both in relation to Barry's version of it (Horton 1996) and in relation to the Rawls's later conception of public reason (Horton 2003), such approaches are more contextually bound and far more indeterminate in their outcomes than their advocates typically allow.[10] However, there is also a more fundamental problem with the whole reasonable rejection argument. This is that the underlying rationale for the reasonable rejection criterion is to be found in the idea of equal respect: that coercing people on grounds that they could reasonably reject is necessarily to fail to show them equal respect. But, as Richard Arneson has rightly observed:

> The problem with the argument from equal respect is that on no plausible interpretation of the norm of respecting other persons will it turn out to be the case that imposing on persons coercively in the name of principles they 'reasonably' reject has to be failing to treat them with the equal respect owed to all persons. (Arneson 2003, p. 213)

This is a point of more general importance, and one to which I shall return below, so I will not say more about it now.

Jones, though, is particularly robust, indignant even, in his response to charges along the lines that there is anything bogus or fraudulent about neutralism. Thus, he writes:

> many of those who complain about the fraudulence of impartiality are unwilling to give up their claims that we should respond to people's differences 'equally' or 'fairly' or 'justly'. But any of these responses must surely incorporate some notion of impartiality. ... [A]mong those who do insist that cultural diversity should be dealt with fairly or justly, I want to claim that the real issue is not whether we should be impartial but what form that impartiality should take. (Jones 1998, p. 39)

And there follows an apparently surprising admission that: 'although impartialist or neutralist approaches are commonly associated with liberalism, the impartiality at stake here need not take a liberal form' (Jones 1998, p. 39). This clearly indicates that impartialism or neutralism need not be liberal; it can take different forms, some of which may be non-liberal. I assume that what Jones has in mind here is, for example, the idea that impartiality per se need not be combined with the promotion of liberty, so that a policy could be impartial but not necessarily liberal, in that it could be quite repressive. But the question that arises in this case is: what is it that shapes or determines these different forms of impartialism or neutralism, if not some broader set of cultural beliefs, values or philosophical assumptions?

At least when I object to liberal neutralism in terms similar to those at which Jones bridles, what I am suggesting is, if not exactly fraudulent, at least misleading, is not the possibility of any appeal to notions such as fairness or impartiality, but the belief that only one specific interpretation – that of liberal neutralism – is justified. Thus, for instance, utilitarianism has its own version of impartiality, even if it is one that neutralist (and most other) liberals would reject, which reflects disagreement about how far and in what contexts numbers should count and about whether the general good should be given greater precedence than individual interests. So, even if the right and the good can be reasonably clearly distinguished, there is no obvious reason to think that there is one uniquely best way in which this must be done. In the context of Jones's discussion of the problem of dealing with cultural diversity, he is surely right that few who have any commitment to facilitating it will advocate that we should do so in ways that are systematically unfair or seriously biased. But, if this is all that is meant, it is no more than a pyrrhic victory, and, furthermore, if as Jones concedes, there are indeed plausible non-liberal forms of neutrality, then perhaps it is not a victory for *liberalism* at all.

I want next to turn, rather more briefly, to Jones's second claim: this is that liberalism requires that there should be no attempt to favour or privilege any particular culture or conception of the good. Perhaps, it might be said, this at least is an uncontroversial feature of any conception of fair treatment that a liberal should endorse. But is it? Although what I have to say about this question is the most tentative of my responses to Jones's three points, I do want to canvass the thought that, even if an argument does seek to privilege one particular culture or conception of the good, that may not be sufficient to make it unfair or illiberal. I emphasize *sufficient* here, because of course it would be absurd to claim that such arguments are never unfair or illiberal; sometimes they clearly are. But it does matter, and I believe that Jones would agree on this point, if this is not *necessarily* true.

It may be helpful at this point to consider an example. It is something of a commonplace that fair treatment of different religions is incompatible with any kind of established church. But, interestingly, this has not been the view of some religious leaders, even when it is their religion that is seemingly disadvantaged. Some years ago, Sir Jonathan Sacks, Chief Rabi of the United Hebrew Congregations of the Commonwealth, argued, to my mind quite plausibly, that he thought that there was nothing wrong with the Church of England being the established religion in England.[11] Indeed, he went further than this in arguing that he thought that it was appropriate, given the country's Christian heritage, and a good thing for religions generally, including Orthodox Judaism, if the alternative was a wholly secular public sphere. He thought it more important that religion had some representation in the public sphere rather than be expunged from it, even if it would not be his religion that was to be favoured in this way. And I have also heard some Muslims argue along somewhat similar lines. Nor is an established church obviously unfair or illiberal with regard to those of a secular disposition, so long as it does not pose a threat to them pursuing their interests and values, and they are permitted to swear non-religious oaths, have secular wedding ceremonies and so on. All I want to suggest is that, even in a highly sensitive area like religion, this is a plausible view to hold; not compelling, but not demonstrably mistaken, or necessarily illiberal, either. And, although, at a stretch, such a view could also be interpreted as an indirect argument for impartiality or fairness – in that it is levelling the playing field with respect to secularism – that is not the only interpretation it can bear, or perhaps the most salient.

If we move from one sort of sublime to another, from religion to opera, then it would appear that the case against this part of the neutralist view is rather stronger. For, it can be argued that there are good reasons for asserting that the opera is a valuable activity, and that these reasons may also be cited in support of state subsidy. These reasons will not be based on claims of justice and nor will they be incontestable; but, crucially, nor do they imply the inadequacy, let alone any moral deficiency, of a life in which opera has no place. There need be no suggestion that a life devoted to other valuable activities is any way inferior to one that includes the kind of musical and dramatic sensibilities cultivated by opera. Indeed, such reasons may succeed in persuading some people who have no interest in opera themselves that it is nonetheless a cultural practice that merits state support, especially if it can be shown (as it surely can) that opera will likely struggle to survive without any subsidy as anything other than an occasional pastime for the very rich. Even if people are not persuaded, however, as some will surely not, and although there is a straightforward sense in which it is unquestionably true that subsidizing opera is privileging one conception of the good over others that are not in receipt of state support, it is far from obvious that those people are being unfairly, let alone unjustly, treated simply because a tiny fraction of their taxes go to support opera. In modern pluralist societies we all pay taxes to support a wide variety of activities in which we have no interest or about the value of which we may be highly sceptical. So long as a decision about what deserves state support is the outcome of some sort of reasonable democratic process then, *ceteris paribus*, there is no reason to hold that anyone has cause for legitimate complaint, whether or not it is a decision with which they agree.

Let us now turn, again only briefly, to the final claim: that so far as possible people should be allowed to live their lives in accordance with their own values and cultures, and should not have opposing, alternative modes of life imposed upon them. In fact, this claim seems to me correct, and one that almost any liberal is bound to take very seriously. Of course, 'so far as possible' is something of a black box, but that is not to the point here, although it might be once the box is opened and its contents unpacked. Rather, the point with which I want to take issue is the implicit but surely wholly egregious assumption that any failure of impartiality or neutrality necessarily undermines either of the two closely related components of this claim. This is because (we are invited to assume) the absence of impartiality does not allow people to live their own lives and also imposes on them an opposing way of life. By contrast, it seems to me, this assumption only has to be made explicit for its implausibility to be self-evident. If we return to the status of the Church of England as the established church in England, I am quite at a loss as to how that prevents believers in other religions or believers in no religion at all from living according to their own creeds. Nor is it any clearer how it is supposed to impose an 'opposing, alternative way of life' on them. And, if we move on to subsidizing opera, then it would seem merely bathetic to make similar claims in this context. Perhaps, if regular opera attendance were made compulsory for everyone, or if opera were so pervasive and utilized so many resources that it undermined other significant cultural options, we might have the beginnings of an argument, but absent of circumstances such as these, it is hard to see how anyone's ability to live their life according to their own values is in any significant way adversely affected by subsidizing opera. Ideas such as 'the imposition of a way of life' or 'preventing people from living in accordance with their own creeds' are wildly inappropriate characterizations of what is going on in such situations. These reflect neither the intent (nor the effects) of state subsidy of opera and much else. To think otherwise, I suggest, one has to be firmly in the grip of an *idée fixe*.

But, perhaps there is a better argument at the root of the neutralist approach that I have not yet properly taken into account? I believe that there is, and it leads us back to a point that was raised earlier: this is the idea that if any of these three conditions is violated we fail to show equal respect to people. Therefore, finally, I want to confront this argument, which is probably the most powerful weapon in the liberal impartialist armoury (see also Steiner 2012). The first point to note is that it is the *equal* in 'equal respect', not merely respect, which does the real work in this context. If we refer merely to respecting others then it is surely clear enough that someone, for example, who thinks that opera is a load of bunk, and would rather spend their time listening to muzak, is not per se disrespected, just because opera is subsidized and muzak is not, even if it is subsidized specifically on the grounds that opera is better than muzak (as of course it is). It is surely possible to respect other people's choices without denying that some choices are better than others. If this were not the case then I suspect that we would be driven to adopt something like an extreme version of the kind of discourse of equal recognition associated with Charles Taylor and others (Taylor 1994), the plausibility of which Jones has himself done so much to undermine (Jones 2006a, 2006b).

Can a similar argument, though, work if we accept that what matters is not merely some measure of respect, but *equal* respect? I think that probably the most meaningful way in which it is possible equally to respect someone's decision to do something or live a life that one believes to be clearly deficient or misguided is in the sense of respecting that it is properly the person's own choice. That is, one accepts that it is her right to choose, and just as much her right to choose for herself as it is for me to choose for myself. Perhaps Jones would agree with this, too. But, if this is right, it does not seem at all apparent that this is inconsistent with allowing that some of the options between which a choice is made can be rendered more or less attractive by, for example, subsidizing some (and taxing others).[12] Nor is it clear why a liberal state should necessarily be prohibited from expressing views about such matters. Does a state necessarily fail to show equal respect to its citizens if it endorses some values or ideals rather than others? It is not obvious that it does: if it examines the conflicting arguments and evidence seriously, accepts that these are not conclusive in that it cannot be shown that it is irrational to hold either view, but nonetheless forms a judgement that the balance of reasons or evidence favours one view rather than another, why must this evince a failure to show equal respect to those who have lost out? Of course, this is not to give *carte blanche* to the state in such matters, but there is no reason to believe that such limits mean it can impose only laws and policies mandated by the supposed requirements of justice. Moreover, there is a serious imaginative failure, I think, if subsidizing opera is thought to be even the same kind of thing (of course any liberal will agree that it is of lesser significance) as, for instance, denying some people freedom of worship.

In short, I suggest that there is no reasonable interpretation of the principle of equal respect that is inconsistent with subsidizing opera on the grounds that it is thought to be an especially worthwhile activity that the state should help to support. This need express no disrespect towards those who show no interest in or attach no value to opera. And it is, for instance, quite consistent with people holding such a view seeking to persuade others that state subsidy of opera is a waste of money, or that the money could be used for better purposes. If those who hold this view can succeed in persuading enough other people then in a democracy it is likely that at some point any such subsidy will be withdrawn. Nobody in this scenario is having a way of life imposed upon them, and in so far as opera depends upon public subsidy to be widely accessible, it is those who value opera who will likely be deprived of the opportunity to pursue one of their values should the state cease to subsidize it. But, of course, nobody should have the *right* to have their values or conception of the good supported by the state; even opera-lovers. My claim is only a relatively weak one, although it is crucially stronger than Jones allows, which is that there is nothing *necessarily* illiberal, unjust or disrespectful about a state supporting some activities because it attaches value to them or wishes to promote them rather than some other activities; it is not the stronger, but unsustainable, claim that any particular values or activities are *entitled* to such support.

III

By way of conclusion, and at the risk of appearing to backtrack somewhat from some what I have argued so far, I want to be clear that it is no part of the argument here that there cannot be any good reasons as to why a liberal might properly object to subsidizing opera. For example, if the subsidy were given in a way that intentionally precluded some groups, on irrelevant grounds, from benefitting.[13] Similarly, it could be reasonable to object to how a subsidy operated on grounds of economic justice, if perhaps it effectively amounted to an unjustifiable subsidy of the rich by the poor,[14] but not merely because some people do not want 'their taxes' to be used in this way. Moreover, I do not want to deny that notions like impartiality and neutrality can have a useful place in a political theory of liberalism, as one important kind of consideration among others. But something has gone seriously wrong with a liberalism that effectively fetishizes one narrow and unconvincing interpretation of neutrality or impartiality, and can seemingly regard it as a kind of litmus test of liberal orthodoxy that the state should not subsidize opera specifically on the grounds that opera is a good thing. Liberals would do better to focus on, as they have done at their best historically, those things that really facilitate or prevent people from living decent, worthwhile lives, so far as possible in accordance with their own views about how they want to live.

In short, it is hard to believe that something like state subsidy of opera, or indeed the intentional and selective favouring by the state of many other particular ideals or conceptions of the good through education, subsidies or other similar means, *necessarily* marks in any important respect a departure from liberal aspirations, simply because such policies are supported on grounds that involve the state taking some values and ideals to be more worthy of its support than others. To suggest that so much hangs on the ideal of neutrality or impartiality so understood is to risk trivializing what is of fundamental importance about liberalism. This is in addition to jeopardizing its robustness as a political theory if it can be shown that the distinction between the right and the good on which that ideal is parasitic cannot be sustained.[15] It is also a much stranger liberalism than its defenders seem at admit that is precluded from promoting any ideals or values that are not strictly matters of justice. Whereas what I want to suggest really matters is that it does not coerce those people who do not share them from having to pursue those values and ideals themselves. There is surely an important distinction between subsidizing opera, through the use a tiny portion of general taxation, and making it compulsory; and liberals should be especially keen to ensure that such a distinction is noted and respected.

Acknowledgements

An earlier version of this paper was presented at the conference held to honour and mark the retirement of Professor Peter Jones at Newcastle University in 2010. I am very grateful to the participants on that occasion, not least to Peter Jones himself, and to Chris Newlove Horton for their helpful discussion of the paper.

Notes

1. This difficulty

    > is whether a state can establish a structure of freedoms without making qualitative choices between different freedoms and between freedoms and other goods. If it cannot the distinction between universal resources and particular goods breaks down and the state faces a choice that intrudes into the area of the good. (Jones 1989, p. 32)

    I agree that this is a problem, but although I do touch on the point below, it is not the main focus of concern here.
2. It is, of course, somewhat unfair to pick on a passing comment in this way, and I would certainly not want to be held to account for every such remark that I have made. I am, therefore, especially grateful to Peter Jones for generously consenting to my using it for illustrative purposes.

3. The idea of reasonable disagreement is not something I have much to say about here, but I have discussed it further in Horton (2009).
4. For a useful discussion of some of these differences, see several of the essays in Montefiore (1975). It is also perhaps worth mentioning that although many of those theorists responsible for introducing the term 'neutrality' have apparently come to regret doing so, this does not mean that they have changed their views.
5. Gerald Gaus offers an especially clear statement of the radical implications of the ideal of state neutrality, arguing that although 'some state action can be justified, it is doubtful whether much in the way of public policy survives the neutrality test' (Gaus 2003, p. 157).
6. For a helpful general discussion of the meaning of 'conception of the good', see Richardson (1990).
7. In a different context Rawls (1999) also remarks that: 'There is no more justification for using the state apparatus to compel some citizens to pay for unwanted benefits that others desire than there is to force them to reimburse others for their private expenses' (p. 250).
8. This does not mean that they are also exempt from other criticisms of the neutralist strategy, including some that I mention in the opening paragraphs of the second section.
9. I do not say much about these constraints in what follows, but as I make clear towards the end, I am not denying that there are such constraints that any liberal should want to see respected with respect to how and on what grounds particular conceptions of the good can legitimately be favoured by the state.
10. This is in part for the very good reason, to put it bluntly, that you only get out what you put in; and what gets put in by liberals (or anyone else) does not exist outside of or apart from *all* contested cultural assumptions and beliefs.
11. Unfortunately, I have been unable to recover the source for this claim, but I believe it was made in a public lecture or radio broadcast.
12. I have focused in my discussion here on subsidy rather than taxation. There are some obvious parallels between the two, but if taxation were also based on disapproval of the activity being taxed, this would introduce a more problematic consideration into the argument, and one that would undermine at least some of the claims that I have sought to defend.
13. The qualification 'on irrelevant grounds' is necessary because it may be entirely reasonable to preclude some groups, e.g. babies and infants or, more controversially perhaps, those with noisy and uncontrollable disabilities that are likely to disrupt seriously the enjoyment of others.
14. It seems that this is potentially the most serious objection to the way in which state subsidy of opera in many states actually tend to work.
15. Among many critcs, Simon Caney, for instance, has argued that

> bearing in mind that even reasonable people are fallible, it follows that to disallow premises which reasonable people dispute may be to disallow sound and correct premises ... [which] will, in some circumstances, prevent the enactment of policies mandated by justice. (Caney 1999, p. 30)

He calls this 'the anti-perfectionist dilemma'. A similar argument is advanced by Arneson (2003).

References

Arneson, R., 2003. Liberal neutrality on the good: an autopsy. *In*: S. Wall and G. Klosko, eds. *Perfectionism and neutrality: essays in liberal* theory. Lanham, MD: Rowman & Littlefield, 191–208.

Barry, B., 1995. *Justice as impartiality*. Oxford: Oxford University Press.

Barry, B., 2001. *Culture and equality*. Cambridge: Polity.

Caney, S., 1999. Liberal legitimacy, reasonable disagreement and justice. *In*: R. Bellamy and M. Hollis, eds. *Pluralism and liberal neutrality*. London: Frank Cass, 19–36.

Dworkin, R., 1985. *A matter of principle*. Cambridge, MA: Harvard University Press.

Freeman, S., 2007. *Rawls*. London: Routledge.

Gaus, G., 2003. Liberal neutrality: a compelling radical principle. In: S. Wall and G. Klosko, eds. *Perfectionism and neutrality: essays in liberal theory*. Lanham. MD: Rowman & Littlefield, 137–165.

Horton, J., 1996. The good, the bad and the impartial. *Utilitas*, 8, 307–328.

Horton, J., 2003. Rawls, public reason and the limits of justification. *Contemporary Political Theory*, 2, 5–23.

Horton, J., 2009. Reasonable disagreement. *In*: M. Dimova-Cookson and P. Stirk, eds. *Multiculturalism and moral conflict*. London: Routledge, 58–74.

Jones, P., 1989. The ideal of the neutral state. *In*: R. Goodin and A. Reeve, eds. *Liberal neutrality*. London: Routledge, 9–38.

Jones, P., 1998. Political theory and cultural diversity. *Critical Review of International Social and Political Philosophy*, 1, 28–62.

Jones, P., 2003. Toleration and neutrality: compatible ideals? *In*: D. Castiglione and C. MacKinnon, eds. *Toleration, democracy and neutrality*. Dordrecht: Kluwer, 97–110.

Jones, P., 2006a. Toleration, recognition and identity. *Journal of Political Philosophy*, 14, 123–143.

Jones, P., 2006b. Equality, recognition and difference. *Critical Review of International Social and Political Philosophy*, 9, 23–46.

Jones, P., 2007. Making sense of political toleration. *British Journal of Political Science*, 37, 383–402.

Kukathas, C., 2003. *The liberal archipelago*. Oxford: Oxford University Press.

Kymlicka, W., 1989. *Liberalism, community and culture*. Oxford: Oxford University Press.

Miller, D., 2012. Grounding human rights. *Critical Review of International Social and Political Philosophy*, 15 (4), 407–427.

Montefiore, A., ed., 1975. *Neutrality and impartiality*. Cambridge: Cambridge University Press.

Rawls, J., 1993. *Political liberalism*. New York, NY: Columbia University Press.

Rawls, J., 1997. Public reason revisited. *University of Chicago Law Review*, 64, 765–807.

Rawls, J., 1999. *A theory of justice*. Revd edition. Oxford: Oxford University Press.

Raz, J., 1986. *The morality of freedom*. Oxford: Oxford University Press.

Raz, J., 1994. *Ethics in the public domain: essays in the morality of law and politics*. Oxford: Oxford University Press.

Richardson, H., 1990. The problem of liberalism and the good. *In*: R. Douglass, G. Mara and H. Richardson, eds. *Liberalism and the good*. New York, NY: Routledge, 1–28.

Steiner, H., 2012. Human rights and the diversity of value. *Critical Review of International Social and Political Philosophy*, 15 (4), 395–406.
Taylor, C., 1994. *Multiculturalism: examining the politics of recognition*. Princeton, NJ: Princeton University Press.
Weale, A., 2012. The right to health versus good medical care? *Critical Review of International Social and Political Philosophy*, 15 (4), 473–493.

Rights as democracy

Richard Bellamy

Department of Political Science, School of Public Policy, University College London (UCL), London, UK

> Like many rights theorists, Peter Jones regards rights as lying outside politics and providing constraints upon it. However, he also concedes that rights are matters of reasonable disagreement and that, as a matter of fairness, disputes about them ought to be resolved democratically. In this paper I develop these concessions to argue that rights require democratic justification and that this can only be provided via a real democratic process in which those involved 'hear the other side'. I relate this argument to the republican theory of non-domination, contending that it fits the Lockean project of regarding rights as constraints on arbitrary power better than liberal views that place rights outside the democratic process. I conclude by noting the implications of this argument for rights-based judicial review of legislation.

Introduction

In his study of *Rights* (1994), Peter Jones takes a broadly liberal view whereby rights stand apart from, and are potentially in tension with, democracy. Although certain rights may be intrinsic to democracy, such as the right to vote, he correctly notes that most rights – among them many of the most important, such as the right not to be tortured – are not (pp. 173–174). Moreover, given that a tyrannous or simply a myopic or misguided majority might democratically vote to allow torture or other rights violations against vulnerable minorities, it may on occasion be necessary to limit democracy to protect rights. Indeed, Jones argues that even intrinsically democratic rights might need safeguarding against a majority that had, for one reason or another, come to embrace anti-democratic preferences (p. 175). As for a right to democracy, he regards such a notion as incoherent given that citizens could reasonably opt for non-democratic arrangements that might protect rights just as well as democratic processes but require fewer commitments or less participation on their part. In fact, partly for the reasons already given, such non-democratic mechanisms might in some cases offer superior and more efficient means for promoting people's rights and other interests (p. 188). In his view, all these caveats to linking rights to democracy reflect 'the traditional political purpose of natural or human or fundamental rights': namely, 'to tell those who wield political power what they may and may not do' (p. 222).

In what follows, I shall contest almost all of these arguments, at least in so far as they apply to established democratic systems. However, I shall do so in part for some of the positive reasons Jones concedes may nonetheless connect rights to democracy – at least contingently. Two of these prove particularly important for my purposes. The first reason concerns the linking of democracy with a concern for fairness. Jones summarizes this position as follows. Taken overall, the decisions of any given political community are likely to have an equal impact on the interests of the individuals who comprise it, giving each of them an equal stake in the political process. If we accept that no individual's well-being is more important than that of any other, and – following J. S. Mill – view each individual as the best guardian of his or her own interests, then democracy will offer the most justified form of decision-making. For 'if individuals interests are equally at stake in a political process, those individuals as a matter of fairness, have a right to play an equal part in that process to ensure their interests are taken equally into account' (Jones 1994, p. 180).

The second reason arises from Jones's concession that rights are subject to disagreement. As he notes, such disputes are not unique to rights but affect all moral thinking to some degree. Typically, following the fairness argument outlined above, we view democracy as offering a legitimate resolution of such disagreements by giving equal weighting to diverse views and producing a decision from them. Yet, Jones (1994) believes 'that way of dealing with dissensus is not uncomplicatedly available to the more ambitious aspirations for rights' (p. 222). If a prime purpose of rights is to constrain the exercise of power so that it does not infringe certain basic entitlements of all human beings, then it seems inconsistent to place such rights within the very political processes they may need to limit. However, as Jones grants, if the content of rights is disputed, then the attempt to impose a particular version of rights from outside such a process will itself 'seem little more than an exercise of power by some over others' (p. 223). We appear to face a practical dilemma, therefore, whereby 'the greater the dissensus about rights, the more practically difficult it will be to establish them as fundamental entitlements which constrain what a society and its government may do' (p. 223). Nevertheless, he believes that 'we should not exaggerate the reality of this difficulty' (p. 223). After all, international conventions on rights exist that can claim the formal adherence of almost all states, while most democracies have domestic bills of rights. He contends these statements of rights command sufficient consensus and, despite their generality and abstractness, are sufficiently action guiding, to allow non-majoritarian bodies, such as courts, to secure their application outside – and occasionally against – the ordinary democratic political process (pp. 223–224). Yet, he admits that general bills of rights still 'leave large areas of discretion open to whoever interprets them and that their interpretation involves judgements of a moral and political rather than a strictly technical nature' (p. 225). As a result, he allows that such issues might, as some rights proponents believe, remain better and more appropriately dealt with by democratic politicians than by unelected judges. Advocates of this view still maintain that 'rights should remain special, but their specialness should be felt in the way they are handled by politicians rather than in their not being handled by politicians' (p. 225).

Jones treats the pros and cons of a democratic as opposed to the judicial resolution of disagreements about rights as largely an empirical and prudential matter. I disagree. I shall argue that the importance of resolving them democratically follows from not only the fairness argument he outlines (but does not ultimately support) for a right to democracy, but also the very nature of rights and the claims we make of others with regard to them. Although not all rights are intrinsic to democracy, I shall argue we assert them most legitimately when we do so in what might be called a democratic spirit: that is, as claims to be treated with equal concern and respect as autonomous individuals within a shared set of collective arrangements.

Rights so conceived can be related to the neo-Roman republican notion of liberty as non-domination as defined by Pettit (1997) and Skinner (1998). Like other recent liberal theorists of rights (notably Dworkin, e.g. Dworkin 1996, Introduction), Jones tends to see at least those rights deserving constitutional protection as best conceived in terms of a right to non-interference by others. That view favours a conception of rights as trumps. However, I shall argue that such a position proves unsustainable. Rights claims will only show citizens equal respect if their views have been equally considered, and only achieve equal concern through collective arrangements that can be shown to track their common recognizable interests – that is, the interests that members of a shared scheme that aspires to treat all as equals could publically avow as being owed to all (Pettit 1999, p. 176). Both these criteria are defining features of liberty as 'non-domination' (e.g. Pettit 1997, p. 56). Both these desiderata also point to something akin to the fairness argument for democracy (Bellamy 2007, pp. 159–175). From this perspective, the link between democracy and rights ceases to be a largely contingent and empirical matter and is rather an inherent feature of their very nature. It establishes not so much a right to democracy as a view of democracy as the foundation of rights. Moreover, this foundation does not consist of some ideal theoretical conception of democracy that might be detachable in practice from an actual democratic process. It requires that rights be proposed and pursued through recognizably democratic procedures that conform to a reasonable condition of political equality.

The argument proceeds as follows. I start by showing how the very nature of a rights claim implies a democratic process in which citizens have the status of political equals when formulating collective decisions that are to apply equally to all. I then relate this democratic argument for rights to the republican conception of liberty as non-domination, rejecting along the way the liberal account of rights as trumps and its origins in a view of freedom as non-interference. Finally, I explore how this association of rights and democracy exists not only at an ideal level but also needs to be actualized within a real democratic process of a kind akin to the systems of actually existing democracies, with their combination of one person one vote, majority rule, and regular elections between competitive parties. For, the normative and logical status of rights as intrinsically democratic in their mode of justification and application greatly circumscribes the legitimacy of using judicial and other non- or counter-majoritarian mechanisms to uphold rights against democracy (Bellamy 2007).

Rights, political equality and democracy

Jones remarks how rights theorists working within the mainstream liberal tradition typically distinguish human and natural from institutional rights on the grounds that the former are in some sense prior to politics (Jones 1994, pp. 72–3). That is to say, they are either moral entitlements that human beings could and ought to be granted even in a putative state of nature, such as freedom from physical assault, or – more demandingly – they encompass those basic interests of human beings that all political communities should seek to secure not just for their members but also for non-members. In other words, such rights should either exist outside of any polity, or be realized within, and upheld by all, polities. As such, they define the boundaries, foundations and to some extent the goals of politics (pp. 75–81).

So conceived, rights readily appear as constraints on democracy. Rights can be viewed as 'trumping' those political decisions that curtail or fail to promote them. Yet, their apparent status as somehow prior to and above politics proves hard to sustain. Rights are sometimes presented as a two-term relation, whereby x has a right to some y. That gives rights a somewhat peremptory sounding character. However, rights are always a three term relation, whereby x asks some z to recognize and respect his or her claim to y, with attendant costs and benefits to z who will wish x to likewise recognize either his or her similar claim to y, or to some other good such as v. That is true even of a Hohfeldian 'liberty-right', whereby all that is being asked of others is that they have 'no right' to prevent its exercise (for a discussion of Hohfeld's classification of rights and of liberty rights in particular, see Jones 1994, pp. 12–14, 17–22). For such forbearance may itself be controversial, as in certain instances of someone exercising a liberty-right to do what might be commonly regarded as wrong (Waldron 1981). Therefore, x and z need to agree on rights and their respective correlative duties, or lack of them, in given situations. It is this need for a collective agreement on which rights we possess, when and where, what their implications may be in a given case, how they interact with other rights, and which policies and procedures might be most suited to realizing them, that places rights within what Albert Weale and Jeremy Waldron have called the 'circumstances of politics' (Weale 2007, pp. 12–18, Waldron 1999, pp. 107–113). For, these are all matters on which we may reasonably disagree yet need a common decision, producing the need for a political mechanism of some kind to resolve our disputes.

Theorists of natural and human rights have tended to assume away such disagreements. They have sought to ground their case for at least a set of basic rights on their 'self-evident' character as dictates of reason, divine law, or essential elements of human well-being (Jones 1994, pp 96–97). Yet, as Jones (1994, p. 97) notes, self-evidence 'is not a very promising foundation for rights'. What leads us to identify specific features of human beings or human sociability as 'natural', 'basic' or 'divinely ordained' depend ultimately on the moral theories we hold for which the specified capacities prove important. The upshot is that appeals to human nature and other supposedly 'objective' and 'universal' foundations of rights reflect rival ontological claims for which no generally agreed epistemology exists with the capacity to mediate between them. As Jones (1994, pp. 224–225) concedes, even where there is agreement on the rather abstract set of general rights found in International Human Rights Conventions or domestic Bills of Rights, there can be disagreement about what they involve in practice with regard to a given case. These disagreements need not reflect self-interest or bad faith – though on occasion they clearly do so, as in the case of regimes whose reluctance to recognize rights results from their oppression of their subject populations. Rather, disagreements – such as one finds in most democratic countries – may simply issue from what Rawls (1993, pp. 55–56) has called 'the burdens of judgement ... the many hazards involved in the correct (and conscientious) exercise of our powers of reason and judgement in the ordinary course of political life'. On Rawls's account, these burdens range from the different life experiences people bring to the assessment of a situation, to the multiple normative considerations likely to be involved and the difficulties of relating them to the often complex empirical evidence. Although he believed these 'burdens' only applied to conceptions of the good, they clearly also produce different understandings of the right. People may reasonably hold differing views of not only the sources and substance of rights, but also their subjects and scope, and how they might best be secured (Bellamy 2001). Thus, Nozickian libertarians,

Ricardian socialists, Rawlsean social democrats and Burkean conservatives all offer different accounts of the origins and extent of property rights and their relationship to other rights, which are expressed to different degrees, albeit usually in a less abstruse or sophisticated manner, in the everyday political debates of all mature democracies. At the level of principle, these disputes have not proved any more resolvable in the seminar rooms of philosophy departments than they have among policy-makers and citizens.

As I remarked, such reasonable, good faith ontological and epistemological disagreements about the nature of rights mean that the determination of which rights we have and how they should be upheld requires a political process. However, not any kind of process will do if it is to be consistent with both the very idea of rights, as something possessed and claimable by all, and the reasonableness of these disagreements about them. In these respects, the fairness argument Jones gives for democracy provides a basis for regarding the democratic process as the most legitimate political procedure for constructing the necessary collective agreement. On the one hand, decisions about rights are ones in which those affected will have an equal stake over the long term and taking into account the full range of decisions. So we need a process that will treat all as political equals in reaching mutually acceptable agreements such as a system of majoritarian decision-making on the basis of equal votes offers. On the other hand, majoritarian voting per se is not tied to any of the arguments – voters can vote for any position and for any reason. As such, it delivers a fair and neutral process for deciding which position can claim the most public support as being in the collective interest (May 1952).

So conceived, the choice of democracy is not, as Jones suggests, purely pragmatic. It follows from the very idea of rights and certain structural features of any claim to a right and the disagreements that will surround it. First, though there are many different arguments for human rights, it is an intrinsic feature of all of them that since rights attach to human beings as such they apply equally to all. Second, and relatedly, although rights connect to individuals we have seen how they have a collective dimension. A right is not claimed solely for the individual in question but as a right that can be held and upheld equally by all other individuals – hence the need for a process to collectively agree on the right. Moreover, for the right to be collectively held and upheld requires not just each individual doing his or her bit according to some commonly agreed norm, but also common, publicly provided, structures – at a minimum a legal system and the means for law enforcement, such as a police force, courts, prisons. So secured, rights function in many ways like what Raz (1986, pp. 198–199) has called an inherent public good: that is, they promote common benefits that we must collectively produce through our attitudes to others and in which we can all equally share – a point to which I return below. Finally, we have noted how rights also operate as claims against those in authority. They imply that certain things should not be done or should not be denied to any individual.

These three aspects of rights point towards a core claim that underpins all rights claims: namely, the claim by each individual to be treated as a political equal who owes and deserves equal concern and respect to and from every other individual in the shared arrangements that frame their social life, a claim that must also be acknowledged by the authorities charged with administering these arrangements. The intimate link between democracy and rights arises from this core claim. For, democracy offers the only forum where different rights claims can be made and the collective structures necessary for their realization can be provided in a way that is consistent with rights claimants recognizing their fellow citizens, with their potentially rival claims, as deserving of equal concern and respect, and ensuring that the public authorities are responsive to their collective disagreements and deliberations about rights. Democracy offers a means for making decisions in which all meet as political equals to make reciprocal claims on each other when framing common policies, and can hold governments to account when they fail to reflect their preferences. In this way, the democratic process grants what Hannah Arendt termed the 'right to have rights'. I am not thereby implying that all rights are intrinsic to democracy. As I noted above, not all rights relate to the democratic process. What I am arguing is that all rights involve a democratic form of justification – they imply a spirit of political equality to be accorded equal concern and respect that can only be achieved through a democratic process.

Rights and individual liberty: liberal and republican perspectives

Seeing rights as somehow intrinsically democratic might be thought to subvert their aforementioned 'traditional political purpose' as identified by Jones (1994): that of telling 'those who wield political power what they may and may not do' (p. 222). However, that perception arises from aligning that 'traditional' understanding of the function of rights with the liberal conception of liberty as non-interference. By contrast, when that purpose is linked to the republican conception of liberty as non-domination – a view that more accurately accords with the nature of rights claims as delineated above – then democracy emerges as a necessary, even if not always a sufficient, condition for its realization. Moreover, whereas Jones aligns the liberal view of natural rights in the 'strong' anti-political sense with Locke (pp. 72, 75) it is the republican tradition that is arguably closer to the 'Lockean' programme (Pettit 1997, p. 40).

Liberalism, rights and freedom as non-interference

The liberal notion of freedom as non-interference seems to capture what many see as the central aspect of rights: namely, that there are certain things nobody should be allowed to do to another individual, such as torture, or prevent them from doing, such as exercising their freedom of speech. Given such rights only require the forbearance of others, they ought to be compossible – able to be held by all others – by their very nature, and so be non-negotiable because not requiring negotiation. Not all rights may be of this kind, but those that are offer some of the most important safeguards for individuals. On this account, there is no role for democracy to play in their formulation or maintenance – as noted above, they may even need to be exercised against democratic decisions.

Rights to non-interference seem the best candidates for being in some sense pre- and possibly anti-political. Indeed, all law becomes inimical to rights in being a form of interference, albeit potentially necessary to render them secure. This approach offers the paradigm of the view of rights as trumps that are held by individuals against the collectivity. Such rights seek to drive a wedge between the right and any notion of the common good, offering pre-conditions for each and every individual to pursue his or her own good in their own way. Yet, even rights of this form cannot be isolated from the 'circumstances of politics'. For they will not be immune from disputes as to their definition; from conflicts between the uses of these rights by different people as well as with other rights; or from the need for the intervention of public laws and collective structures to realize them. All these issues prove political in the broad sense noted above. For, they require a collective decision over the content and scope of these rights that will rest on value judgements concerning their purpose and nature – the public good or goods they serve – that allow for reasonable disagreement.

Thus, there may be agreement that no one should be tortured and all authorities and individuals should simply refrain from doing so, but interpretative disputes nevertheless exist as to whether certain punishments shade into torture or not – think of the arguments in the United States over whether the death penalty is per se 'cruel and unusual' or only certain methods for delivering it. It might be countered that though the practical meaning and implementation of this right are political, the right itself is not – it is a moral right that attaches to individuals as something one simply should not do to any person – hence the aforementioned agreement that torture is wrong. As I noted above, though, the moral force of even the most basic human rights does not follow from our humanity per se but the moral theory we hold, and people can and do have different views about the morality of torture, not all of which are rights-based. These differences will always prove relevant because the circumstances in which even a right such as this arises is always political to the extent that the claim is made against other persons and requires institutions or at least an agreement to be reliably enforced among them. There is no right of the individual as such, but only of the social individual within a political and legal context (Bellamy 2010, pp. 416–420). Indeed, the historical origins of a right not to be tortured lie not in an absolutist view that this right ought to be upheld whatever the consequences, but because it was regarded as ineffective as a means for extracting evidence and corrupting of those who employed it. It was the general utility of torture as a means for upholding the rights of the public, rather than the right of an individual regardless of its impact on the public, that led to its abolition (Beccaria/Bellamy 1764/1995). A political agreement on the public meaning and the good served by this right, as well as the best means to uphold it, are neither additional to nor potentially at odds with the nature of such a right: they are essential to its definition and justification.

Similar debates arise in the case of free speech and whether incitement or libel count as 'speech' in the legally acceptable sense.[1] These involve uses of the right to free speech that potentially subvert other rights of individuals, as is the case with slander, hate speech or the leaking of official secrets. Such conflicts indicate that though many rights may appear simply to depend on an absence of interference, making them available to all will require intervention by public authorities to facilitate their use and guard against their abuse or subversion. It might be argued that we should simply seek to interfere as little as possible with the right in question so as to maximize its availability to all. Yet, what counts as interference is normatively laden (O'Neill 1979/1980), as are the choices of what arrangements might maximally enhance a right in given circumstances. Some will regard certain omissions as well as acts as forms of interference, for example, or see threats and intimidation as potentially as inhibiting as physical force, others will not. Likewise, some might see an equal right as requiring no more than an equal chance to exercise it, such as might be achieved by a lottery, others that it be exercisable to an equal extent – with both views proving highly contestable even in their own terms, especially when it comes to establishing them in practice.

In collectively evaluating the nature and limits of rights and providing common means for their realization, as we have seen is necessary, the right comes to fall within, rather being separate from and potentially opposed to and 'trumping', the common or public good. For the rights that will be viewed as commanding the equal concern and respect of all citizens will be those that correspond to their commonly avowable interests and that therefore provide an equal benefit to all. Indeed, not to align rights with the public good in this way has the perverse effect of making rights seem like the privileges of particular individuals rather than the universal entitlements of all citizens – an aristocratic rather than a democratic view. As Raz (1994, p. 54) has noted with regard to free speech, issues such as libel and slander make it implausible to see free speech as the right of each and every individual to say whatever he or she wants regardless of its more general effects on the rights of others. It also seems odd to suggest that we have an interest in this right for our own personal use as individuals, say in order to vent our frustrations in monologues delivered in front of the bathroom mirror – satisfying though this may be on occasion. It is also the case that few of us are likely to be opinion formers or whistle blowers either. So we do not necessarily have a personal interest in exercising this right ourselves. Rather, we all have an equal interest in the benefits of free debate and criticism of public policy by the comparatively small group of people with the time and expertise to do so – politicians, journalists, those with specialist knowledge in a given area and so on – and in the possibility to join that group being equally open to all, including ourselves should we feel motivated to do so. An equal right to free speech is thus instrumental to securing a public good rather than distinct from any such good. Hence, the common rules and structures that we favour for regulating free speech are those that we believe best serve that public purpose – for, these are the rights all should and could have. Once such structures are in place, their role is to provide an equal and common benefit for all rather than a privilege for an individual to indiscriminately berate his or her neighbours or business rivals out of spite or for personal profit.

Republicanism, rights and freedom as non-domination

Rights, then, cannot be removed from politics. Instead, we need a form of politics that is consistent with their character. As we saw at the end of the first section, rights involve a core claim to be treated with equal concern and respect – both by one's fellow citizens in the shared arrangements that coordinate social life, and by the public authorities empowered to oversee them. Consequently, a political process for collectively claiming and deciding on rights will need to possess three key features. First, it must show equal respect for the different views of individuals as rights bearers. Second it should also demonstrate equal concern for their capacity to employ their rights on the same terms as others. As such, it will need to be doubly collective – a process that involves all the public on an equal basis and promotes those rights and conceptions of rights that best reflect commonly avowed interests. Third, it will have to answer to the 'traditional purpose' of rights as means for holding power to account and marking its limits.

Unlike the classic liberal view of freedom as non-interference, the republican notion of non-domination captures this core claim underlying rights by offering a normative basis for these three requirements of a justified rights generating political process. On this account, freedom and rights belong not to an asocial agent outside all social and institutional arrangements and able to do what he or she wants because of the lack of interference with or by others, but rather is a civic achievement of socially situated individuals whose relations are regulated by law. What gives these legal arrangements their liberty preserving quality lies in them being formulated by free and equal citizens who are not bound to any master but rather negotiate their collective arrangements together as political equals in order to arrive at policies that serve the common good rather than the partial and potentially dominating interests of particular powerful individuals or factions. The rights that arise from these arrangements still reflect the ways in which citizens tell those in power what they may or may not do. Yet, citizens achieve that 'traditional purpose' through claiming their rights through laws that apply equally to all – including their rulers – and which they ultimately control though a democratic process that shows each of them equal concern and respect as autonomous individuals.

Freedom as non-domination is not inimical to politics and law in the same way as freedom as non-interference (Pettit 1997, ch. 2). Its aim is to achieve freedom from the arbitrary rule of a master rather than freedom from any rule. Rights play a part in that achievement, but they are the rights of citizens not the natural rights of human beings that could be held either outside of any society, or as members of any society. Rather, they result from the laws that citizens give themselves as equal members of a polity. Arguably, this republican position fits the Lockean project rather better than the liberal account. Jones characterizes the Lockean tradition as committed to the upholding of natural rights as the primary task of government. In that case, though, Locke would have regarded law as a constraint on rights, to be kept to the minimum necessary to secure them. However, that is not his view (Pettit 1997, p. 40). As Locke/Laslett (1681/1965) noted, 'freedom from Absolute, Arbitrary power' is the goal of a good polity, with law an essential part of that given 'that ill deserves the Name of Confinement which serves to hedge us in only from Bogs and Precipices ... the end of Law is not to abolish or restrain, but to preserve and enlarge Freedom' (pp. 325, 348). True, Locke does mix this republican language with jurisprudential natural rights thinking. However, as these quotes suggest, he is perhaps best read not as using rights as fundamental norms in the liberal, deontological sense – except perhaps for rhetorical reasons – but as legal norms that arise from and promote freedom as non-domination (Pettit 1997, p. 101).

The view of rights as existing outside and potentially against politics, and hence able to trump a democratic process, overlooks how rights are claims made by citizens on fellow citizens within a social and political setting. Two key errors flow from this oversight. First, it ignores the fact, explored above, that the rights claims of one individual impact on those of other individuals. As we have seen, rights do not attach to human beings as such within a putative state of nature. They belong to and reflect a given social context and the public goods it provides for those who exist within and support it. An individual claiming a right is not the only person possessing trumps. All those he or she he is claiming against possess trumps too. The trumping metaphor ceases to be useful in this context. At best, one can argue that there are some especially weighty claims that individuals may have that need to be weighed in the balance with the similarly weighty claims of other individuals. Second, these trumps have already been played in the democratic process where we decide what rights the legal system should enshrine within the relevant legislation (Waldron 1999, p. 12). Legislators and indirectly those who have elected them can all express their views on rights in framing legislation, and seek to have their most basic interests and core views protected. All effectively play their trumps, but only on the same terms as everyone else. Therefore, in making a claim against a democratic decision, the rights claimer is illegitimately attempting to play his or her cards again, and in the process is failing to treat his or her fellow citizens with the equal concern and respect rights demand.[2]

What, though, do we do in the case of those who do not have access to any or to the relevant democratic institutions – who either live in non-democratic states or outside a given democratic state, be it as a stateless person or as a citizen of a different state – yet have a claim against the democratic decisions of a state that has adversely affected them? Surely, human rights claims often arise in their most powerful and urgent forms precisely in such situations, where either no democratic redress is available or democratic processes have ignored the interests of those excluded from them. Indeed, many established democratic systems have excluded certain members of the political community in the past – women, those without property, ethnic minorities, among other groups – and many continue to do so. All of this is undeniable. And yet, the claims such groups make can be seen primarily as claims for inclusion within the democratic community – to be treated as political equals. Far from overlooking the claims of the excluded, the republican account has decided advantages over the liberal in this regard. For the liberal view can be used by the privileged to mandate such exclusions to prevent unjustified interferences with their entitlements – be it the property rights of the rich or the sovereignty of wealthy states. By contrast, the republican view mandates inclusion as a political equal within the decision-making processes of those powerful bodies capable of exercising domination over our lives. These may be public bodies – the state or its agencies – or private bodies, such as large corporations or financial institutions. The liberal language of human or natural rights leaves the unprivileged outside the city walls, as mere petitioners for redress by the privileged within, who may deploy these self-same rights to deny any civic responsibility for these others. The republican approach brings all rights-claimants within the city walls, giving them access to the political mechanisms required to offer them redress. Yet that brings the obligations as well as the privileges of citizenship – not least the duty to take the rights claims of others as seriously as they take their own. Unsurprisingly, the evidence shows that rights will only be reliably upheld where the democratic mechanisms exist for them to be claimed in this way, and that rights are just as reliably ignored and infringed where such mechanisms are absent (Christiano 2011). It is to the specific virtues of actually existing democracy that we now turn.

Rights and democracy: real and ideal

A number of theorists have acknowledged the democratic character of rights in framing their accounts in terms of an idealized democratic process – be it the rights that must be presupposed by free and equal dialogue or discourse with another, or those that would be agreed to, or could not be reasonably rejected in, circumstances where all participants are equally situated with regard to each other and none has power over another. This democratic argument for rights has been most explicitly stated by Jürgen Habermas (e.g. Habermas 1998, ch. 10). Yet a parallel argument also informs John Rawls's *Political Liberalism* (1993), where he characterizes his first principle of justice as reflecting an agreement between idealized citizens of a liberal democratic state as the necessary conditions for them to co-exist as political equals (p. 3). However, this idealized democratic argument for the foundations of rights does not necessarily entail a practical commitment to use real democratic systems to uphold them. First, both Habermas and Rawls seek to distinguish constitutional from normal politics, regarding the more general and public debate they associate with the one as legitimately constraining and providing the norms underlying the other (Habermas 1996, pp. 304, 486, Rawls 1993, pp. 232–233 – for a critique, see Bellamy 2007, ch. 3). Second, both see constitutional courts as exemplifying a more ideal form of democratic discourse than real democratic processes. Habermas (1996, pp. 263, 278–279) argues that courts can review democratic decisions on procedural grounds to ensure they have issued from a duly democratic process, while Rawls (1993, pp. 157, 161) maintains they may review them on substantive grounds as well to ensure that certain non-democratic rights have not been infringed, thereby removing certain rights from politics altogether. Finally, and as a corollary of this last point, both see litigation as a form of democratic participation.

This section challenges and qualifies all three of these arguments. I shall argue that idealized, court-based democracy is no substitute for real democracy. If political equality is necessary for all to be treated with equal concern and respect as both the claimers and the duty bearers of rights within the circumstances of politics, then no purely ideal account of democracy can substitute for real democratic practices and participation. Such ideal theories risk being entirely circular, construing the democratic process so that it favours their preferred view of rights. Nor can any abstract theory be so specific as to incorporate all the features that figure within actual contexts – not least the very diverse life experiences and concerns of those involved.

I shall start by outlining the constitutional qualities of normal democratic politics. The superiority of real democratic systems over courts lies in their providing a mechanism for identifying the legislative embodiment of rights most likely to track the commonly avowed interests of citizens by treating them with equal concern and respect. It achieves that result through providing a means for citizens to reach agreements in conditions of political equality. On this account, so-called normal politics is constitutional politics, for it allows the on-going legislative enactment of rights in the democratic terms required to justify and legitimately realize rights claims. I then turn to an examination of courts and argue that far from offering a more ideal version of this process, courts lack the fundamental democratic quality of allowing an equal input from all affected citizens – their 'right' to author their rights. Nor can their interpretation of a constitutional document that may at some stage have had democratic legitimation in a referendum be regarded as offering a democratic basis for their judgments, isolated as these are from the democratic views of the current citizenry. Meanwhile, the distinction between procedural and substantive review proves hard to sustain. Not only are the rights inherent to a democratic process as contentious as those that lie outside it, with the latter (as I noted) often more basic and important than the former, but also judgements on what counts as a due process turn to a considerable degree on views of the nature of an appropriate outcome. However, if the courts cannot provide a forum for what Pettit (2000) terms 'authorial' democracy, they can provide a venue for what he calls 'editorial' or contestatory democracy for those groups that may not have had voice in the democratic determination of the right. Litigation can play a democratic role here. However, such 'editorial' democracy is necessarily weaker than, and subordinate to, 'authorial' democracy – it offers the basis for a weak form of judicial review that can be overridden by the legislature.

The authorial merits of real democracy

Democratic systems have undeniable defects and though they can be improved must always be expected to fall short of the ideal. However, much the same can be said of any human institution – including courts. So, in advocating courts as correctives for the mistakes of democratically elected and accountable executives and legislatures it is necessary to bear in mind the mistakes that they will also make. The key question has to be whether courts possess practical and normative qualities that render them more likely to uphold rights and to do so in more justified ways than democratic systems might do? In posing this question, I do not wish to deny that courts and democratic mechanisms have various complementary qualities, with each being best supplemented by the other – a point I return to below. However, their complementarity per se is not at issue here. Rather, the central point is which should have constitutional supremacy in defining whether rights have been upheld or not. Political systems, such as the United States, which have strong rights-based judicial review, hand over that decision to a supreme or constitutional court which can disapply laws they believe infringe rights. But many other systems – such as the UK and Nordic countries like Finland and Norway – have traditionally had far weaker forms of judicial review and give more power on these matters to legislatures and special parliamentary committees. In what follows, I shall argue that the use of these legislative as opposed to judicial mechanisms for rights protection can be justified not just on pragmatic grounds but also for normative reasons to do with the democratic character of rights. For these normative arguments can never be embodied as fully in judicial practices as they are in legislative ones.

As I have argued elsewhere (Bellamy 2007, ch. 6), the key constitutional quality of actually existing democratic systems arises from their combining majority rule with a dynamic form of the balance of power that results from electoral competition between parties. This combination allows such systems to meet the requirement for political equality demanded of a republican notion of freedom as non-domination, thereby allowing rights to be considered in ways consistent with equal concern and respect, on the one side, and the blocking of arbitrary uses of power by those in government, on the other. Majority rule offers a fair decision procedure for resolving disagreements that gives all involved an equal voice, thereby satisfying the need for equal respect. Electoral competition in societies typified by cross-cutting cleavages, and where the main policy differences can be plotted on a left–right continuum, obliges voters indirectly and politicians vying for power directly to 'hear the other side', thereby meeting the requirement for equal concern. For, to build a majority, parties – or coalitions of parties – must bring together the preferences of as many different groupings among the electorate as possible. The result is that the rival party blocks tend to converge on the median voter, which usually represents the Condorcet winner on a pair wise comparison of the various policy preferences of the electorate as a whole (Ordeshook 1986, pp. 245–257). As research on the relationship of party manifestos to government policies has shown (Klingermann et al. 1994), within democracies that have these characteristics there is a reasonably high correlation between the electoral campaign and the legislative programme of the successful parties. Moreover, governments in such systems inevitably operate under the shadow of the coming election, and so remain accountable to shifts in electoral opinion. They have an ever present incentive to formulate polices that are non-arbitrary because they track public interests – those that will coincide with respecting the views of most citizens and addressing their common concerns as far as possible.

In this scenario, the prospects of any tyranny of the majority are low (McGann 2004). Those who lose consistently will be groups at the extremes of the political spectrum, who have failed to modify their views sufficiently to be able to link up with other sections of the electorate. It is not that their rights have been denied, for they have had the right to express their views on which rights ought to be available and in what ways (Tushnet 1999, p. 159). Their opinions about rights and the interests that lie behind them have been treated on an equal basis to everyone else's. However, they have not managed to convince their fellow citizens that their view of rights would treat all those affected by its implementation with equal concern and respect And that failure largely results from not heeding the equally important rights claims of a sufficient number of their fellow citizens, so that the costs and benefits of any collective policy on rights can be shown to be fairly shared by all.

This argument will not satisfy a rights theorist who holds that rights attach to individuals outside of any social or political arrangements and should be respected regardless of their costs to others. However, the previous section showed this position to be self defeating, since it involves a violation of rights itself. The justification of any rights claim needs to be on the grounds that it offers an equal recognition of the mutual rights claims of those others who will have the correlative duty to uphold it. Given disagreement about rights, the best available way of mediating between rival claims is via a fair process in which each person's views is treated on a par with everyone else's and there is encouragement for all to accommodate the preferences of everyone else so far as they can. As we saw, such a process can be regarded as reflecting the democratic spirit that lies at the heart of any reasonable rights claim. It also provides a means for realizing freedom as non-domination. For it attempts to allow only those interferences that track common avowable interests – that is those interests that can be avowed politically as showing those involved in a shared social scheme equal concern and respect through functioning as a public good in the sense mentioned earlier. What I have now argued is that actual democratic systems offer a realistic approximation to such a rights promoting process.

Courts as unreal democracy

Nevertheless, there will certainly be occasions when democratic mechanisms – either inadvertently or otherwise – do not treat all interests equitably or accommodate certain key concerns sufficiently. Certain persons affected by collective decisions may be excluded from the decision making process altogether, or be ignored by others due to prejudice or because they are too small and dispersed a group to have any hope of being able to organize themselves so as to be electorally significant. Electorates may also act myopically or be misinformed. In any democratic system there is also the possibility that certain constituencies may prove to have disproportionate influence or others none at all, with the result that electoral decisions may register false positives or false negatives. In these situations, many have thought courts might offer a legitimate safeguard against democratic failures – not least because their processes can claim a certain democratic legitimacy of their own.

Two related claims are made in this regard. First, it is claimed that courts – especially constitutional courts – employ a form of public reasoning and deliberation that is more truly democratic than a standard electoral process. Judges are not only trained to apply the law impartially, so that it applies equally to all, but also are bound to justify their arguments in terms of constitutional rights norms that themselves reflect the up shot of an ideal democratic process – the norms – roughly speaking the main liberal civil and political and even certain socio-economic rights – that anyone who accepted democracy would regard as necessary to secure participation as an equal within the public sphere broadly construed. The judiciary's independence from electoral pressures means they are less swayed by the need to pander to popular prejudices. Instead they can ask whether legislation could be regarded as consistent with a publically justified reading of these rights. As I noted, this argument may be interpreted in either a substantive manner, as relating to the outcome of democratic decisions (Rawls 1993, lecture VI, Dworkin 1996, Introduction), or in a procedural manner, with regard to the processes by which democratic decisions are made (Ely 1980, Habermas 1996, ch. 6). Second, it is held that litigation is itself a form of participation. In particular, it allows legislation to be contested on the basis that it fails to meet the standards of equity and fairness inherent to democracy by giving those unable to get an adequate hearing in the regular political process a chance to voice their concerns (Kavanagh 2003).

Both these claims for courts to offer a better and more ideal democratic forum for the authorship of rights than real democracy can be challenged. For a start, we have seen that constitutional rights norms can be subject to reasonable disagreements, especially when applied to particular cases. Given that the decisions of multimember courts are often made on the basis of a majority vote, the judiciary can clearly disagree as much as the rest of the population. Yet, their disagreements need not be representative of, or responsive to, the electorate as a whole. That might be no bad thing if we had grounds for regarding their disagreements as somehow resulting from more 'rights-responsive' reasons to those of the general public. But it is not obvious why that should be the case. The fact that they refer to rights in their reasoning does not of itself necessarily mean that their views of them are especially conscientious, better informed, or less biased than other people's. In fact, they may well be less so than politicians who precisely because they need to engage with the views of the electorate have to be aware of the impact of a particular way of interpreting and implementing rights on the lives and interests of those they represent. Each citizen's views may be partial, but the nature of the electoral contest makes politicians views rather less so as they have to appeal across the board. By contrast, the danger is that the views of the judiciary are simply arbitrary from the public's perspective – they are merely the views of those individuals on the bench.

It will be objected that judicial reasoning is constrained by precedent and law. However, neither of these constraints per se can be regarded as necessarily producing a more objectively correct view of rights. If there were a clear methodology for arriving at the right answer on moral questions, then there would no longer be such disagreement about these issues – but no agreed method exists. At best, we have rival methods, each of which tends to exist in a circular relation to the view it wishes to promote. Meanwhile, not only is precedent a notoriously weak constraint – especially when dealing with hard or novel cases of the kinds that typically give rise to judicial review, but also it and legal reasoning more generally may in so far as they do apply be inappropriate constraints. If courts are tied by precedent, then that implies a status quo bias that hinders those cases that might rightly challenge previous decisions. Likewise, the only parties and considerations a court can consider are those that have legal standing in the case at hand. But when deciding public policy it is often necessary to consider the knock-on effects for a wide range of seemingly unrelated policies. Moreover, not all the relevant moral issues involved need be best articulated in terms of rights. Indeed exclusive focus on the way a right has been legally defined may subvert a full discussion of the question at hand. Think of the distorting effect of arguments about the right to free speech that focus on whether a given form of expression can be characterized as 'speech' or not.

Some theorists have argued that these difficulties can be overcome by a procedural approach to judicial review (Ely 1980). As Habermas (1996) puts it, 'a constitutional court guided by a proceduralist understanding of the constitution does not have to draw on its legitimation credit' – it can leave the substance of rights to a democratic process and confine its views to simply adjudicating on whether democratic decisions respect the 'logic of argumentation' (p. 279). Yet, he defines valid procedures in terms of 'the communicative presuppositions that allow the better arguments to come into play in various forms of deliberation' (pp. 278–279). A 'consistent proceduralist understanding of the constitution relies on the intrinsically rational character of a democratic process that grounds the presumption of rational outcomes' (p. 285). In other words, the test for judging the rationality and appropriateness of a given democratic procedure rests on whether it produces rational outcomes. This argument simply undermines the procedural-substantive distinction. As with other rights, rights related to the democratic process need to be claimed and reformed within existing, normal democratic politics. For example, it is through such mechanisms the workers and women gained the right to vote in the United Kingdom, that forms of proportional representation were introduced in New Zealand and in the UK for regional and European elections and so on. Compare these dramatic and progressive changes with the blocking of similar measures in the United States by successive judgments of the Supreme Court (for details, see Bellamy 2007, pp. 107–129).

What about the potential of litigation as an additional forum for democratic participation and contestation? Partly for related reasons, it may fail or be worse in this respect too. Litigation will only be possible for those parties that the court views as having a case in law. So it is a restricted forum, the terms of which are controlled by the court. As we saw, these controls may be such as to hinder rather than facilitate new or hitherto excluded voices getting heard. Then there are the resource problems of going to court. Access to justice is costly and time consuming, and cases can take years to be heard. That can often favour those with deep pockets. Given that all citizens start with an equal vote, there is the danger that courts enable illegitimate double counting, with those who cannot muster sufficient popular support to win in politics shopping in an alternative forum that is less open and hence more favourable to the position of privileged minorities or sectional interests.

As a result of these defects courts, like legislatures, can register false negatives and positives as well as legislatures (Bellamy 2009). But this practical weakness is not entirely symmetrical to that found in political processes. Though those who get to court may be treated equally with regard to the law, by contrast to the political system they cannot claim their rights to equal concern and respect on their own terms as political equals. The terms whereby they get access to the law are always the law's, and in these sorts of cases the tribunal they must address is not one of their peers but the judiciary who are set above them as those who determine the state of the law on the case in question. The difficulty lies in the very constraints needed to give individuals a fair trial under the law by impartial judges can make courts inappropriate forums for considering the public good aspects of rights and ensuring that they show equal concern and respect to all those not represented within them. The insistence on legality, on the one side, and independence from extraneous influences, on the other, aim to ensure judges make decisions as far as possible free from personal bias, financial inducements or fear of reprisals from those sympathetic to one or other of the parties. Yet, the common good aspects of rights may involve considerations beyond the law in question and require a responsiveness to the consequences for the public at large. Court's engaged in rights-based review typically deal with such questions under the heading of 'proportionality'. Yet unlike legislatures they lack the feedback mechanisms likely to ensure such judgments are well-informed. Governments have to respond to the votes of millions of citizens and their assorted needs by presenting them with a programme of government and have both the opposition and several hundred representatives seeking re-election from their diverse constituencies to remind them of that fact. For good reasons, courts are isolated from such pressures.

Courts and editorial democracy

It will be pointed out that not all litigants in human rights cases are tobacco companies contesting restrictions on advertising in the name of free speech or film stars protecting their ability to sell their wedding photos to the highest bidder in the name of privacy. There are also asylum seekers, prisoners, the mentally ill, immigrants and other unpopular or isolated minority groups, with limited if any access to the democratic sphere. Even if not all deserving cases get to court and not all those that do so are decided well, there is at least the prospect that some of those individuals whose rights will go unregarded otherwise will get a hearing. For these cases, courts can offer a legitimate avenue of contestatory democracy. While the constraints typical of courts make them a poor authorial forum, they prove well suited as supports for an editorial forum. Courts seek in their own proceedings to ensure that litigants are treated impartially with regard to the settled norms of the law. In doing so, they apply notions of equity and procedural fairness. As a result, they are highly attuned to adjudicating on the issue of whether a given party to a dispute has been given an adequate hearing or if the norms governing a case have been interpreted even-handedly to all parties. In cases where a litigant, such as an asylum seeker or a prisoner, could show that his or her position had failed to be treated equitably in either of these ways, then contestation of the authorial decision seems legitimate with the courts an appropriate forum. The issue then becomes how strong can such contestation be before it merges into a less legitimate form of authorial democracy?

Some accounts of editorial democracy, such as Pettit's – at least in some formulations – see a written constitution and bill of rights as offering the authorial basis for such editorial contestation (Pettit 1999, 2000). However, that overlooks the fact that the electoral branch may have claimed to offer these as much attention as the judicial and sought to legitimately reinterpret them so that they accorded more truly with the current views and interests of people with regard to certain issues. If a court is allowed, as under strong contestatory review, to strike down legislation or to read into it its own reading of its fit with constitutional norms, then it is in effect usurping the authorial function of electoral democracy. By contrast, a weak form of contestation allows courts merely to question the compatibility on the fairness grounds outlined above and to force a reconsideration by the legislature. In many respects, the British Human Rights Act can be read in such terms as a form of 'weak' contestatory judicial review (Bellamy 2011). Under this scheme, the rights enumerated under the Act remain an ordinary piece of legislation that the electoral branch can alter if it deems that necessary. However, in the meantime it seeks to ensure its current legislation is compatible with such rights norms and to mark when it seeks, for reasons it deems legitimate, to depart from them. Yet courts can dispute whether it has done this sufficiently thoroughly and ask the legislature to reconsider – though how and when remains the prerogative of the authorial branch of democracy. Here democracy – real democracy – remains the authorial foundation for rights, with the courts offering a supplementary function as an editorial alarm bell.

Conclusion

Jones sees rights as distinct from and potentially constraints upon politics. They are a means for preventing illegitimate interferences with individual liberty. Democracy offers at best the most appropriate mechanism for upholding them. But that is only because of the empirical flaws of the alternatives and of our reasoning about rights, not due to the very nature of rights themselves. By contrast, I have argued that rights involve an implicit appeal to democratic forms of reasoning. Moreover, this inherently democratic character of rights is best captured by a republican view of liberty as non-domination, rather than the standard liberal account of liberty as non-interference. Nevertheless, this republican view can still capture 'the traditional political purpose of natural or human or fundamental rights', and arguably offers a more accurate account of the 'Lockean' programme than the liberal's. Nor is this account simply an ideal view of the relations between rights and democracy, that itself has only a pragmatic relation to actually existing democratic processes. The only justifiable authorial foundation of rights must be some form of on-going democratic decision making that allows rights to be claimed under conditions of political equality. At best, courts provide the basis for a weak form of contestatory or 'editorial' democracy that draws attention to neglected or otherwise unheard voices. However, the only legitimate final say on rights rests with the people themselves, among whom the benefits and burdens of rights must equally fall as commonly avowed goods that serve their shared interests.

Acknowledgements

Earlier versions of this paper were presented at seminars at the universities of Frankfurt, Newcastle, Edinburgh, Florence, Libera Università Internazionale degli Studi Sociali Guido Carli (LUISS) in Rome, and the Institute for Historical

Research in London. I am grateful to John Ferejohn, Philip Pettit and Jürgen Habermas; Peter Jones, John Horton and David Miller; Martin Loughlin, Neil Walker, Chris McCorkindale and Matthias Krumm; Quentin Skinner and Richard Bourke; Furio Cerutti, Luca Baccelli and Emilio Santoro; and Gianfranco Pellegrino, Nicola Lupo, Marco Olivetti and Giorgio Pino, respectively, for their helpful comments on these occasions. I also wish to thank Rowen Cruft, Andreas Niederberger, Ian O'Flynn, Philipp Schink, Laura Valentini and Albert Weale for valuable written comments.

Notes

1. There is the additional issue of how a right, the exercise of which appears simply to involve forbearance, can nonetheless clash with its similar exercise by others. We regard rights as important not only for a single individual, but also for all individuals. If a right to free speech is to be collectively exercised we will need rules of order so we do not always all speak at once so that nobody can be heard above the cacophony. Of course, this point does not generalize to publishing or the media, which are the most important cases of free speech today, but it is a difficulty with the exercise of certain other rights, as when a successful entrepreneur gains a monopoly through the exercise of free market rights that may inhibit their future exercise by others.
2. It could be argued that all can also have resort to law on an equal basis to everyone else. However, access to courts not only tends to be more restricted and costly than the exercise of a vote, but also courts offer a narrower forum. The only parties that have standing are those that have standing in law, so that a much narrower range of considerations are debated. If the aim is to justify rights in public terms as reflecting common avowable interests, then the judicial arena cannot achieve this. At best, it allows citizens to argue that their commonly avowed interests have not been considered appropriately in the legislation – a contestatory purpose that is explored in the following section, but which does not justify a strike down power on the part of the courts. I have discussed these points at length in Bellamy (2007, ch. 1).

References

Beccaria, C., [1764] 1995. *On crimes and punishments*. Ed. R. Bellamy, Cambridge: Cambridge University Press.

Bellamy, R., 2001. Constitutive citizenship vs. constitutional rights: republican reflections on the EU Charter and the Human Rights Act. *In*: T. Campbell, K. D. Ewing, and A. Tomkins, eds. *Sceptical essays on human rights*. Oxford: Oxford University Press, 15–39.

Bellamy, R., 2007. *Political constitutionalism: a republican defence of the constitutionality of democracy*. Cambridge: Cambridge University Press.

Bellamy, R., 2009. The Republic of Reasons: public reasoning, depoliticisation and non-domination. *In*: S. Besson and J.-L. Marti, eds. *Legal republicanism: national and international perspectives*. Oxford: Oxford University Press, 102–120.

Bellamy, R., 2010. Dirty hands and white gloves: liberal ideals and real politics. *European Journal of Political Theory*, 9, 412–430.

Bellamy, R., 2011. Political constitutionalism and the Human Rights Act. *International Journal of Constitutional Law*, 9, 86–111.

Christiano, T., 2011. An instrumental argument for a human right to democracy.

Philosophy and Public Affairs, 39 (2), 142–176.
Dworkin, R., 1996. *Freedom's law: the moral reading of the American Constitution*. Oxford: Oxford University Press.
Ely, J.H., 1980. *Democracy and distrust: a theory of judicial review*. Cambridge, MA: Harvard University Press.
Habermas, J., 1996. *Between facts and norms*. Trans. W. Rehg. Cambridge: Polity.
Habermas, J., 1998. *The inclusion of the other*. Cambridge: Polity.
Jones, P., 1994. *Rights*. Houndmills: Macmillan.
Kavanagh, A., 2003. Participation and judicial review: a reply to Jeremy Waldron. *Law and Philosophy*, 22, 451–486.
Klingermann, H.-D., Hofferbert, R.I., and Budge, I., 1994. *Parties, policies and democracy*. Oxford: Westview.
Locke, J., [1681] 1965. *Two treatises of government*. Ed. P. Laslett. New York, NY: Mentor.
May, K., 1952. A set of independent, necessary and sufficient conditions for simple majority decision. *Econometrica*, 10, 680–684.
McGann, A.J., 2004. The tyranny of the supermajority: how majority rule protects minorities. *Journal of Theoretical Politics*, 16, 53–77.
O'Neill, O., 1979/1980. The most extensive liberty. *Proceedings of the Aristotelian Society*, 80, 45–59.
Ordeshook, P.C., 1986. *Game theory and political theory*. Cambridge: Cambridge University Press.
Pettit, P., 1997. *Republicanism: a theory of freedom and government*. Oxford: Oxford University Press.
Pettit, P., 1999. Republican freedom and contestatory democratization. *In*: I. Shapiro and C. Haker-Cordón, eds. *Democracy's value*. Cambridge: Cambridge University Press, 163–190.
Pettit, P., 2000. Democracy: electoral and contestatory. *In*: I. Shapiro and S. Macedo, eds. *Designing democratic institutions*. New York, NY: New York University Press, 105–144.
Rawls, J., 1993. *Political liberalism*. New York, NY: Columbia University Press.
Raz, J., 1986. *The morality of freedom*. Oxford: Clarendon.
Raz, J., 1994. *Ethics in the public domain*. Oxford: Clarendon.
Skinner, Q., 1998. *Liberty before liberalism*. Cambridge: Cambridge University Press.
Tushnet, M., 1999. *Taking the constitution away from the courts*. Princeton, NJ: Princeton University Press.
Waldron, J., 1981. A right to do wrong. *Ethics*, 92, 21–39.
Waldron, J., 1999. *Law and disagreement*. Oxford: Oxford University Press.
Weale, A., 2007. *Democracy*. 2nd edition. Basingstoke: Palgrave.

The right to health versus good medical care?

Albert Weale

Department of Political Science, School of Public Policy, University College London, London, UK

> There are two discourses that are used in connection with the provision of good healthcare: a rights discourse and a beneficial design discourse. Although the logical force of these two discourses overlaps, they have distinct and incompatible implications for practical reasoning about health policy. The language of rights can be interpreted as the ground of a well-designed healthcare system stressing the values of equality and inclusion, but it has less application when dealing with questions of cost-effectiveness. This difference reflects the distinction between the deontological status of rights claims and a teleological approach presupposed in the language of beneficial design. However, the value of the separateness of persons contained in the discourse of rights can impose constraints on the adoption of a simple maximizing principle when thinking about the allocation of healthcare resources within a social contract for health. Throughout these issues are discussed by reference to the work of Peter Jones.

Introduction

The problem with which this paper is concerned can be simply stated. Influential currents of thinking since the signing of the United Nations Declaration on Human Rights in 1948 have asserted that there is a human right to health and that all persons possess this right. Let us for the moment accept this way of talking. Now consider an alternative way of talking in which we assert that a good healthcare system is one that secures comprehensive, high-quality care available to all those eligible for its services without financial barriers to access. In characterizing a civilized healthcare system in these two ways, we have clearly expressed ourselves differently. But are these two ways of speaking simply different ways of making the same point, or are they logically and theoretically incompatible with one another? I shall call this question the 'compatibility problem'. To characterize this problem, I shall say that it is a question of the compatibility between a 'rights discourse', on the one hand,

and a 'beneficial design' discourse, on the other. When we use the language of rights, we appear to be asserting what is morally right treatment in respect of individuals; when we use the language of beneficial design, we are considering how to balance different values in the design of an institutional arrangement to common advantage among the members of a political community. How, if at all, are these two ways of speaking related?

The view I shall propose in this paper offers a modest, though important, role for the concept of a human right to health in any justifiable account of the design of just healthcare systems. In proposing this account, I draw support from the fact that although Peter Jones has always wanted to defend the place that rights thinking has in our moral and political deliberation, he has never sought to over-inflate that thinking or burden it with logical and conceptual features that are too heavy to bear. In consequence, much of my analysis will reflect lessons that I have learnt from him, in particular the understanding of modern human rights as specifying in a more expanded form the content of traditional accounts of natural rights, as well as the idea that the function of rights is to assert the moral standing of persons thereby denoting what they are entitled to simply as persons.

It may be urged that the problem with which this paper is concerned, whilst theoretically intriguing, is of little practical relevance. In practice, it might be said, talking of the right to health simply provides a framework within which the performance of different healthcare systems can be evaluated. Thus, in a comprehensive report on countries' attempts to secure the right to health published in *The Lancet* (Backman et al. 2008), the notion of a right to health is simply used as an umbrella term designating those features of healthcare systems (a national plan, adequate data, constitutional provisions, non-discriminatory access, participation and so on) that are assumed to lead to good-quality healthcare for all. In a similar vein, Michael Freeman (Freeman 2009) has noted how the UN Special Rapporteur on the right to health has interpreted the right as a requirement according special priority to victims of discrimination, indigenous peoples and those who have suffered from stigmatized conditions like mental illness and disability.

It seems churlish to quarrel with this use of rights discourse in a policy context. Those evaluating policy are less concerned with the underlying logic of the institutions and practices they are examining and more intent on focusing on how well those institutions and practices are performing by reference to identifiable criteria. The rhetorical and persuasive advantages of being able to rely upon the language of rights, language that is legally recognized in international treaties, should not be underestimated when pursuing a good cause in a hostile world. From this point of view, to worry about the compatibility of two ways of speaking about desirable features of healthcare systems is otiose. Philosophers only interpret the world; the point is to change it.

There is much with which to agree in this critique, but also much with which to disagree. Empirical questions of institutional design are central to realizing rights. We cannot just read off from the notion of a right to health a reliable account of how best to organize healthcare, and *a priori* reasoning is no substitute for empirical evidence. Much may depend on the social, institutional and cultural context within which human rights are interpreted and enforced. Thus, to take one example from *The Lancet* study, we cannot assume that having the right to health constitutionally recognized is a relevant or meaningful indicator of improvement in the performance of healthcare systems. A good example of the untoward possibilities of constitutionalizing a right to health is provided by Rueda's (2010) account of the changing jurisprudence of the Colombian Constitutional Court during the 1990s. The 1991 constitution had strengthened the mechanisms of judicial review and created a writ for the protection of fundamental constitutional rights known as the *tutela*. According to Rueda's analysis, this resulted in a 'top-down' extension of social rights to the poor and the marginalized deriving from by the Court's use of the concept of *minimo vital* between 1992 and 1998. However, when economic crisis hit Colombia in the late 1990s, the middle classes were able to use those same legal powers to protect their economic and social rights, including the right to healthcare in a way that the poor were not. The constitutional provisions thus worked as a device for maintaining social inequalities and economic privileges, not ending them. The example illustrates how in practice the language of rights may be deployed by different groups of actors for politically incompatible ends. To change the world for the better requires us to interpret it with care.

So, on the assumption that there is a real problem to discuss, I shall proceed as follows. Firstly, I shall seek to identify more clearly the terms of the potential incompatibility between talking of the right to health and talking in terms the characteristics of a good healthcare system. Secondly, I shall examine the extent to which the language of rights helps us define the grounds of healthcare provision as well as the standing of persons within that provision. However, and this is the third point, the absolutist language of rights is less suitable for dealing with questions of relative priority in the context of a concern for cost-effectiveness in healthcare than the language of institutional design. Fourthly, we can still employ the idea of rights to define what is involved in a fair share of benefits in a scheme of collective mutual insurance, and in this way we can define the terms of a social contract for health, a contract that is between utility and rights. The value and limits of rights, a constant theme in the work of Jones, are thereby exhibited in the case of healthcare.

Defining the incompatibility

There are a number of declarations of the right to health in international law. Article 23 of the UN Declaration of Human Rights says:

> Everyone has a right to a standard of living adequate for the health and well-being of himself and of his family, including food, clothing, housing and medical and necessary social services, and the right to security in the event of unemployment, sickness, disability, widowhood, old age or other lack of livelihood in circumstances beyond his control.

(All quotations of international covenants and agreements come from Brownlie 1981.) The same article goes on to claim special care and assistance are entitlements of motherhood and childhood. Similarly, the 1959 UN Declaration of the Rights of the Child asserts that children are entitled to grow and develop in health. The 1966 UN Covenant on Economic, Social and Cultural Rights is the most explicit when it says in Article 12: 'The States Parties to the present Covenant recognize the right of everyone to the enjoyment of the highest attainable standard of physical and mental health'. That same article then goes on to list some of the steps that are necessary 'to achieve the full realization' of this right including: provision for the reduction of the stillbirth-rate and of infant mortality; improvements to the environment and industrial safety; preventive medicine in the field of epidemic control and other diseases; and the creation of conditions in which all medical services are available in the event of sickness.

These claims are only the most explicit ones about the right to health. Other rights found in international law, including the right to life and the right not to be tortured, also imply serious responsibilities in respect of health. Even international agreements that do not assert a right to health make interesting references to the protection of health. Thus, the European Convention on Human Rights does not contain a right to health, but it does assert that the protection of health is a valid reason for suspending or modifying the force of other rights, for example the right to private property (Article 8). So in this regard at least, within the European Convention considerations of health provide powerful reasons on a par with rights, even though no right to health is as such claimed.

In these examples of international law, the ascription of the human right to health of all individuals is taken to imply a duty on governments to ensure that the right is secured, whilst recognizing that resource constraints mean that full protection of the right will not achieve the 'highest attainable standard'. Thus, what governments ought to do is bounded by what they can do. (There are difficult issues lurking here about the integrity of judgements some governments offer for lack of attainability that I will not go into.) However, although the duties appear to fall primarily upon governments, there is no reason, as part of the logic of rights, to deny that other actors also acquire duties as a result of these rights. For example, in respect of occupational hazards to health, employers may come to have a duty arising from the right to health to provide a clean and safe workplace. There are also interesting questions as to what duties citizens have towards one another as a result of the right to health, for example whether the parents have a duty to ensure that their children are vaccinated in order to prevent the spread of contagious diseases. Yet, however the duties arising from the right to health are thought to ripple out to actors beyond the state, the logic of the international rights treaties seems to be one in which duties arise, whoever might be the duty-holders, as a result of the rights that are ascribed to human beings as such.

The duties on governments to ensure environmental protection, provision for occupational health and safety as well as preventive medicine also imply recognition that there are non-medical ways to improve health. Such measures have high importance in developing societies, where improved sanitation and water supply, as well improvements in nutrition, are essential in improving population health (O'Neill 2002). However, despite the importance of public health and environment measures in both developing and developed societies, I shall be concerned in the rest of this paper with medical care. The allocation of resources through medical care systems raises a number of distinct problems, and no one contemplating, say, the political controversy in the United States over President Barack Obama's healthcare plan could assume that the issues of principle involved in such care were trivial.

How are we to understand the right to health theoretically? In particular how far can we understand its force and plausibility using the philosophical theories of rights that have been developed in modern analytic political theory?

To cast a political claim in terms of rights is generally thought to make a difference to the way in which practical reasoning about public policy should be conducted. To assert that there is a right not to be tortured or a right to a fair trial is to place a constraint on governments to which they would not be subject if it was simply said that it was a good thing for people not to be tortured or unfairly detained in prison. To respect rights is to weigh them heavily, perhaps even pre-emptively, against other social and political values, a feature that Dworkin's (1977, p. xi, *passim*) metaphor of rights as trumps brought out nicely but which is also to be found in Raz's (1990, pp. 35–48; 1986, pp. 186–187, 195–196) account of exclusionary reasons as well as other theories (Jones 1994, pp. 53–56). In respect of the right to health, if acknowledging the force of asserting that right is to make a practical difference to the way in which resources are allocated, then we shall need to consider the implications of this pre-emptive feature of rights talk. A right is not just another value to be realized but a moral constraint to be respected or the ground of some overriding duty upon governments in pursuit of their ends.

Consider now the alternative way of thinking about a good medical care system, namely the 'beneficial design' perspective. Suppose we say that a good medical care system is one that supplies high-quality, comprehensive healthcare without financial barriers to access to all members of a political association (Weale 1998). Each of these elements carries implications about the institutional design of a medical care system. Thus, to say that the healthcare is high quality is to say that the system is one in which medical services are not simply confined to meeting minimal standards of service, but rather has the goal of providing care that embodies high standards of professional practice. Moreover, to say that this is a feature of the *system* of care is to draw attention to the need to make the general level of care received by any patient as good as can be. Aneurin Bevan claimed that the aim of the UK National Health Service (NHS) was 'to universalise the best'. Taken literally this aim is strictly speaking unattainable, since there is always variation in professional performance and achievement. Yet, as an aim, it points to a policy ambition to ensure the provision of care to all members of a political community is the best that can be practically secured.

To say that the care is comprehensive is to say that it covers not simply a limited number of conditions, but is in principle aimed at treating any illnesses for which there are available medical procedures. To be sure, there are difficult practical and ethical questions about what constitutes illness and how treating illness can be distinguished from enhancing normal functioning. Thus, most people would say that pharmaceuticals to increase athletic or examination performance were enhancement rather than healthcare, whereas treatment for rare or even mild conditions was healthcare. Yet, there are many troubling instances between enhancement and cure: teeth whitening, tattoo removal, baldness, and so on. In some circumstances a case can be made for the inclusion of all or any one of these as a part and parcel of healthcare properly so called. However, although these issues can raise important practical questions in each case, for the purposes of comparing discourses we can work with an intuitive understanding of what a comprehensive service would involve in terms of the range of conditions that it would cover.

The principle that there should be no financial barriers to access precludes a two-tier system of care with some members receiving high-quality care because they can pay and others minimum or merely adequate care because they cannot pay. As such, the principle does not imply 'free at point of use', although this is the normal interpretation given for the UK's NHS where no charge can be made for care unless it is specifically mandated by Parliament. Other systems by contrast, for example those of France and Norway, routinely charge for certain services. Yet the practice of charging does not itself imply a breach of the principle of no financial barriers to access. In policy terms it is a nice problem as to how to set charges in such a way as to avoid a deterrent effect. However, as a matter of principle, there is no reason as such why some forms of charging at the point of use should not be compatible with test of there being no financial barriers to access.

How does it come about that we have these two different ways of thinking about what a good healthcare system involves? One possible answer is that we are using two sets of concepts at different stages of practical reasoning. We use the language of rights to refer to the value and force of the claims of individuals to receive adequate medical care. We use the language of design to provide criteria to assess the degree to which the right is being realized in practice. On this account, speaking of the right to health is a way of making a moral claim, whereas speaking of quality, comprehensiveness and access are ways in which we judge how well institutions are meeting the demands of that claim in the way in which they function. The difficulty with this resolution, however, is that using the language of rights as the ground for a moral claim involves a form of moral reasoning that carries distinctive implications about the status and standing of individuals within a political order. Human rights, by definition, carry special weight against the claims of social goods in general, otherwise their assertion would not have pre-emptive force.

More generally, a rights discourse and a beneficial discourse rest upon different conceptions of society. The rights perspective starts with the idea of human rights from which it derives the duties that are incumbent upon governments either to respect rights or to promote them through the provision of certain services. The institutional design perspective is based on a conception of society as a cooperative practice for mutual advantage among its members, and the task is to find institutions that advance the common interests of those members. From this point of view, the challenge is to write the terms of a social contract that will successfully advance those common interests in particular respects. In the case of medical care, the fundamental reasons why principles of institutional design are needed is that a market in health insurance suffers from certain well-known defects of cost-escalation and quality assurance as well as the particular importance attached to health as a dimension of human welfare. From this perspective, thinking about a good healthcare system is less a matter of individual rights and more a matter of collective determination of the institutions necessary to achieve desired outcomes (cf. White 1995, pp. 24–27, Bellamy 2012). Whereas the rights perspective rests upon a theory that is deontological in character, stressing the strength of certain claims upon political authority, the beneficial design perspective is teleological seeking to advance the common ends of citizens through the creation of forms of social cooperation. To see these differences more clearly, it is useful to trace out the meaning and implications of taking rights as the grounds of medical care provision.

Rights as grounds

'Individuals have rights, and there are things no person or group may do to them (without violating their rights).' So wrote Nozick (1974, p. ix). This is to conceive of rights as grounds or reasons for action or restraint. Such an approach is a natural mode of thinking about the role of rights discourse in a political morality, and it is consistent with the way in which classical social contract theory works (with the usual bow to Hobbes for his originality in parsing the logic in such a way that everyone having a right to freedom in the state of nature means that there is nothing each cannot do to others). Such an account of rights naturally goes with a deontological approach to political morality and a political theory in which limits are placed on state action, as is indeed the case with Nozick.

However, there is another side to the story, as Jones (1994, p. 86) suggests. He notes that successive declarations of rights have tended over time to expand the content of those claimed rights. Thus, Hobbes and Locke referred to the rights to life and liberty. Subsequent declarations have expanded their content to include things such as the right to a fair trial or a level of personal security. If we take this approach, how might we understand the right to health? If it is defined as the right to the highest attainable level of health by means of the institutions of a modern medical care system, then one interpretation is that the right to health is simply being expanded in content in the same way as statements of other rights have been expanded. Moreover, the right to health may itself be thought of as an expansion of the right to life. The character of the right is not being changed, but its implications are being spelt out in a particular historical and institutional context, just as we might say that the right to personal security was being spelt out by reference to police resources, even though classical natural rights theorists lived before the invention of the police force. This is a possible way of approaching the problem, but in the case of health (and perhaps also personal security) it leads directly back to the compatibility issue. For, once we try to think about the content of those institutional arrangements that putatively realize the right to health or personal security, we require a beneficial design mode of thinking, since the details that are taken to expand the content of the right specify particular institutional characteristics.

Another way of thinking about the force of rights claims is to focus not on what it is that the right is a right to, but rather on the standing of those to whom rights are ascribed. It is a striking feature of the UN Declaration that the phrase 'everyone has a right to …' or its equivalents figure repetitively in the specification of the designated rights. So the logic of the claim to rights is one of moral equality, inclusiveness, non-discrimination and common humanity. As the opening preamble of the UN Declaration puts it, the declaration is being made in 'recognition of the inherent dignity and of the equal and inalienable rights of all members of the human family …' as the foundation for freedom, justice and peace. If the use of rights discourse is to capture this way of thinking, we move away from a focus on how to think about the content of individual rights towards the idea that to ascribe a right is to assert a set of entitlements or form of moral standing. This enables us to take advantage of Jones's own account of rights as titles (offered by way of modification to the benefit and choice theories), in which he points out that the possessor of a title becomes 'the locus of legal or moral concern' (Jones 1994, p. 36).

If we focus on this element of rights discourse, then we can find some compatibility between a rights approach and a beneficial design approach, since we can make the right to health a constraint on the design of healthcare institutions. From this point of view, a medical care system would be illegitimate if certain classes of persons or groups were excluded from its benefits. The right to health means that no one in a political association should be subject to a test of access that does not apply to everyone in that association. The public authorities must craft institutions that give all associates equal standing. To talk of individuals' right to health is a way of talking about social and political equality as it bears on medical care. From this point of view, the right to health is a way of underlining the importance of there being no financial barriers to access to comprehensive and high-quality medical care.

There is much to be said for this interpretation of rights discourse, both in terms of political morality in general and in terms of understanding the UN Declaration in the historical circumstances in which it was drafted. If one is formulating a declaration against a background of holocaust and genocide, then an emphasis on the dignity of all human beings carries great political force. Even in well-developed and well-functioning modern healthcare systems there are still good reasons for taking this element of rights discourse seriously, say in relation to health services for homeless persons, refugees and travellers, groups that are not easily incorporated in the bureaucratic processes that modern medical systems require. However, taking the right to health as underlining the importance of there being no financial barriers to access either in general or with particular reference to vulnerable groups makes the claim of right just one element in a beneficial design discourse rather than the basis of a freestanding claim.

In this context, a proponent of rights discourse could say that the claim of a right to health is in part a claim about the priority that health as a good should occupy in our way of thinking. There are many things other than health that count as goods. However, there are few of these goods to which we are willing to ascribe a right to their enjoyment. Now doubt it is a good thing if people have pleasant housing, enjoyable holidays, smooth-running electrical gadgets, an ample library and a well-stocked wine cellar. But none of these things can be described as rights, in the way in which we might think it was good to be free from pain, anxiety and disease. The basis for this ascription of rights can vary, but one way of grounding such an ascription is to stress the extent to which health is a 'primary good' in the earlier Rawlsian sense that this is the sort of good it is rational to want, if one wants anything at all (Rawls 1999, p. 54).

However, the problem with attaching the language of rights to a claim about the priority of health is that, whereas a long and healthy life is typically a necessary condition for achieving one's plans and purposes and so can be regarded as a primary good, the highest attainable state of health is not a primary good in this sense (cf. Griffin 2001, p. 25). To the extent to which enhancing one's health conflicts with other goods one might pursue at the individual level, then it may make sense to increase the risk of ill-health or disease as a way of achieving those other goods. Driving, playing dangerous sports and travel will all seem good to some people, and they will pursue those goods at the risk of ill-health. Collectively a similar logic applies. To the extent to which investing in the best that medical science can provide conflicts with other collective purposes, then there is no reason to think that healthcare has absolute priority over other goods. And, if it is urged that a conflict can occur with other goods that we regard as rights (personal security, a fair trial and so on), it is equally true that sacrificing those rights is normally only justifiable when they conflict with other rights, not when they conflict with things it would be merely good to have.

A final way in which one might give a distinctive role to the idea of the right to health is to note that it is intended to be a pre-institutional right, in the sense that it is supposed to provide a reason to shape institutions in a particular way, rather than being conditional upon institutional arrangements. This feature seems to have special significance when we consider the international obligations that the members of a society have towards other societies. Clearly, if we consider the present state of the world, it is global inequalities in health that are its most conspicuous feature. Where there is famine, malnourishment, large-scale preventable disease, it does seem to make sense to say that certain human rights are being violated, or at least to say that the weight of interests involved provides strong reason for other agents to take action to ensure that the right is satisfied. Another way of putting the point would be to say that one reason for thinking that global inequalities are a form of injustice, rather than simply being an unfortunate by-product of economic and social activities, is to do with the adverse effects of those inequalities on the health of many people.

In this context Wolff (2012) makes the important point that one reason for taking seriously the claims of a right to health is that the cost constraints limiting the provision of medical care in poor societies are not simply facts of nature, but may themselves be policy variables to be altered or changed. For example, the price of pharmaceuticals depends upon the pricing policies of pharmaceutical manufactures and the willingness or otherwise of those manufacturers to supply products at different prices to different markets. There are examples of successful interventions where manufacturers have been persuaded to alter their pricing policies to make products more accessible in poor societies. One value of a rights discourse, then, is that it enables us to provide a critical perspective on current or prevailing institutional arrangements, without taking for granted how fixed those arrangements are.

One can accept this way of thinking without, however, being driven to the thought that rights discourse is decisive in understanding such issues. If dealing with global inequalities is ever going to go beyond ad-hoc transfers in the case of emergencies, then it will presumably require institutionalizing the sort of collective responsibility for the financial risks of ill-health that characterize modern medical care provision, having put in place adequate public health measures to deal with water, sanitation and other environmental threats to health. In this context, precisely the same issues of balancing values that characterizes the beneficial design perspective will arise. In other words, once one goes beyond the obvious duties associated with the relief of suffering and disease of a serious sort, and starts to move towards 'the highest attainable' state of health the usefulness of rights discourse falls away.

The requirements of cost-effectiveness

Behind these limitations on the value of rights discourse when applied to medical care there lies one important fact. The language of rights is ill-suited to dealing with the setting of healthcare priorities, where it is a matter of evaluating the relative claims of individuals and groups to treatment rather than detailing the standing that individuals have as equals either within a form of political association or in the world at large. Between two persons with the same right to health, there is no ground for determining priority in the face of scarcity. More particularly, if persons have the right to health, it is hard to see how someone could be denied treatment where that treatment was extremely expensive. When dealing with the need to determine priorities in healthcare allocation, the logic of cost-effectiveness is at odds with the logic of rights, but the logic of cost-effectiveness is closely tied to the setting of healthcare priorities.

The policy dilemma of cost-effectiveness can be simply stated. Medical technology is such that there are many interventions that secure a small or modest improvement in health status at great expense. For example, a number of current and anticipated anti-cancer pharmaceuticals yield only a few months' increase in life span at considerable expense. In these circumstances, the principle of cost-effectiveness says that the public funding of medical care should only extend to those interventions that meet a suitably defined cost-effectiveness test in which the benefit of the intervention is set against the cost of securing it. Yet, whereas the principle of cost-effectiveness sits well in the framework of a beneficial design way of thinking, it fits less well with the idea of a right to health for a number of reasons. To see why not, we have to consider how cost-effectiveness in healthcare allocation is currently conceived.

An influential way of thinking about cost-effectiveness in healthcare is expressed by the use of the idea of a 'quality-adjusted life-year' (QALY). Although this can be complex to operationalize, it is conceptually relatively straightforward. The approach begins with two assumptions. The first is that the benefit provided by a medical intervention can be measured by the increase in life expectancy it is likely to yield. The second is that quality of life is an important component of measuring benefit, so that added years of life should be quality-adjusted. A QALY is then a year of extra life scaled to reflect the quality that year of life typically possesses. So defined QALYs can be used to evaluate the gain that an intervention delivers. The cost-effectiveness of any particular intervention can be assessed according to the number of QALYs it produces for a given expenditure. Thus, if two interventions produce the same increase in survival rates for the same cost, but the second also delivers a higher quality of life as measured by freedom from pain or better social functioning, then the second constitutes a better buy than the first. The ratio of QALYs gained to expenditure incurred becomes the crucial test of cost-effectiveness.

It is routine procedure in the UK – and in this regard the UK is viewed by a number of other countries as a model – to assess healthcare interventions by a cost-effectiveness test that relies upon the definition of a 'good collective buy' as being a figure of £20,000–30,000 per quality-adjusted year per person of survival for any particular intervention. That is to say, if the cost of an intervention to extend a life of a full QALY value is at or below this range, then the intervention will be funded. If it is above this value, the general rule is that it will not be funded, although that decision will be finally made depending upon the particularities of the issue in question. This threshold has been developed by the UK's National Institute for Health and Clinical Excellence (NICE) (2008). It is not applied mechanistically, but it is used to discriminate between those therapies that should be funded and those that should not be. In other words, the test of cost-effectiveness leads to some interventions not being funded, even though they yield some positive healthcare benefit, because the ratio of cost to benefit in QALY terms is above the relevant threshold. What are the theoretical implications of using such a test of cost-effectiveness for our understanding of the right to health by contrast with the beneficial design approach?

In terms of beneficial design, there is a clear sense in which a test of cost-effectiveness compromises the values of comprehensiveness and high quality. High-quality care may be expensive care, and a test of cost-effectiveness will limit the availability of high-quality care. There are specialist physicians who argue, for example, that NICE is depriving cancer patients of the best care that is available because of the funding limits that it imposes through the use of a QALY-based test (e.g. Sikora 2007). By a parallel argument, the same can be said of comprehensiveness. Just as that use of QALYs means that there are some conditions in which the best technically available treatment is precluded by cost, so there may be some conditions in which there is no treatment at all, other than palliative care, because any treatment is too costly according to the ratio of expenditure to benefit. But compromise is not sacrifice. Any institution set up to realize certain values will sometimes find that those values conflict in their design specifications, and the task is to find a reasonable balance among the relevant values. By contrast, the approach of rights is to require that rights be satisfied before other values are pursued, otherwise the rights do not have pre-emptive force. In other words, the beneficial design approach makes individual entitlements the outcome of a set of decisions about optimal design, in which the rights of individuals represent the benefits they derive from the designed institutions and practices. Within the framework of a rights discourse, institutional design is constrained to respect the rights of individuals. From this perspective, although it may turn out in practice to be hard or impossible to respect rights in particular cases, this is not to say that institutions should be designed so as to deny rights to persons as an intrinsic part of their set-up.

The similarities and differences between the right to health and the right to a fair trial are illuminating at this point. Some have argued that just as the public authorities have the duty to provide for fair trials, so they have a duty to provide medical care to meet the standard of the highest attainable health. By contrast, there is a line of argument in the literature on human rights in which a logical and normative distinction is drawn between negative rights – those constraining what the public authorities and other individuals may do, for example they may not torture – and positive socioeconomic rights – rights that requires specific action on the part of the public authorities, for example establishing a healthcare system. Yet, as has often be said in defence of the idea of socio-economic rights, there is no valid contrast between such rights and civil rights, such as the right to a fair trial, solely on the grounds that the former involve expenditure and the latter do not, since clearly courts and legal administration have to be paid for, so even 'negative' rights incur costs. From this point of view, justice and healthcare are just two of the services that governments provide in order to protect and enhance peoples' rights.

However, one can accept this similarity between positive and negative rights without thinking that there is no contrast at all. In particular, we need to distinguish the case where cost considerations compromise the right and the case where cost considerations void the right. To say to people that they were not entitled to a fair trial merely because it was too expensive to provide the court services would not make sense. Although under certain conditions it may be impossible to assure a fair trial on cost grounds, the inference we should draw in such cases is that it had proved impossible to secure the right to a fair trial given resource constraints, and the right had been compromised. However, in the case of healthcare, the argument is not that the right to health is being denied on grounds of cost. It is that people do not have a right to certain treatments when they are too expensive. The claim to the right is void. In the case of a fair trial, the design of the relevant institutions is made conditional upon an assignment of the relevant rights; in the case of the right to health, the assignment of entitlements is made conditional upon the rules that specify the institutional practice.

In this vein, it has been argued by Dworkin (2000) that some form of cost-effectiveness is compatible with just healthcare, and hence a respect for persons, since it would be a 'disservice to justice' for some citizens to expect other citizens to pay for cost-ineffective care. If this argument could be made good, then there would be less of a problem in reconciling the idea of a right to health with the practice of imposing limits on what can be afforded. Presumably one cannot have a right to a good that it would be unjust to require others to supply, so any argument to show that cost-effective care is *ipso facto* just healthcare looks promising in the present context. Yet the force of this argument depends upon having a workable criterion for deciding what counts as a just claim to cost-effective care. Dworkin believes that he has such a criterion, by reference to a set of conjectures about how individuals would insure themselves in a hypothetical fair insurance market. Thus he imagines prudent individuals in their early adult years having to take out insurance policies to cover the financial risks of ill-health. Such prudent individuals would insure themselves against the health costs arising from a wide range of contingencies but not insure themselves, for example, against 'heroic and expensive treatment that could prolong their lives by only a few months' (Dworkin 2000, p. 315). Since for Dworkin just healthcare expenditure is given by the sum of the willingness to pay of individuals in hypothetical fair situations of choice, it is easy to see why, if some things would not be insured by individuals themselves, it would be a disservice to justice to force everyone to pay within a mandatory scheme.

The trouble is that this approach is liable to the same criticism that Dworkin himself levelled against Rawls's use of contractual choice behind a veil of ignorance (Dworkin 1977, ch. 6). It is difficult to see why anyone should feel themselves bound by the putative outcome of a hypothetical decision. Moreover, other than assertion, it is impossible to know what rational individuals would insure against in a possible world remote from our own. Thus, suppose those in need of expensive healthcare maintain that their right to health is being violated by a denial of therapy on cost-effectiveness grounds. They could argue either that the contingency in which they find themselves is one that prudent hypothetical individuals would insure themselves against, or even if such individuals would not so insure, that decision has no bearing on their own entitlements.

There is another way in which it might be argued that there was no denial of rights in excluding the public funding of cost-ineffective medical care. This is to note that any expenditure on one person means less for someone else. Highly expensive interventions of low effectiveness thus potentially impose loss of service upon a large number of people in the form of the opportunity cost of the resources used. This is especially so in any healthcare system in which there is a maximum cash-limited amount to be spent and divided among the population, but it is true to some degree in any modern healthcare system in which there is the pooling of risk. It is a principle of responsible citizenship that one is accountable for the resources one takes out of the economy, and for one person to demand of others that they suffer in order to relieve his or her suffering is to fail to be accountable in a fair way. From this point of view, the cost-effectiveness test preserves a fair balance among a set of potential recipients of healthcare, and there can be no right to claim more than one's fair share.

However, this argument is not as clear as it might seem at first sight. Those who are familiar with the philosophical literature on 'should the numbers count?' will know that there is long-standing discussion of the role of relative numbers in the determination of what makes for right action, sparked by Elizabeth Anscombe's (Anscombe 1967) stout defence of the view that the numbers should not count, since, if fewer rather than more people are saved, then those in the more numerous group have no right to complain that they have been wronged. There is no need to take sides in this dispute to realize that a simple assertion that a large opportunity cost implies that individuals do not have rights is too simple a view to take. The problem is not an easy one to resolve in the beneficial design perspective, but there is little traction gained in securing an answer from the mere invocation of there being an opportunity cost associated with any intervention.

There is one further difference in the conceptual features of the two approaches that takes us to the heart of the potential incompatibility between them. In a beneficial design approach, there is no reason to assume that it is possible to satisfy all three *desiderata* of quality, comprehensiveness and no barriers to access simultaneously, even in wealthy societies. Seeking to ensure high-quality care, together with comprehensiveness and absence of financial restrictions can form an inconsistent triad, where the different elements come into conflict with one another through the need to reconcile conflicting claims on resources. It is in the nature of any design that desirable features cannot all be realized simultaneously. By contrast, in setting priorities, a rights perspective seems ill-suited to the compromises involved because rights claims presuppose a certain universalizability. The central use of rights claims is to make demands on agents such that the right holders can simultaneously exercise their claims. Thus, in principle, all can be assured the right of no imprisonment without trial or the right of freedom of movement, although under particular circumstances there may be conflicts. This is the significance of the claim that a rights assignment should be consistent with the compossible exercise of the rights assigned (Steiner 1994, pp. 33–41, 86–101, 190–194). By contrast, in terms of access to medical care resources, there is a built in problem of scarcity, since resources allocated to one person are not available to others.

It might be argued that there was no inconsistency between applying a cost-effectiveness test and asserting a right to health, since the right is phrased as a right to the 'highest attainable' healthcare rather than a right to healthcare as such. However, attractive though it would be to adopt this solution, it will not work. Highly expensive healthcare – that is to say, healthcare that both has a low cost-effectiveness ratio and costs a lot absolutely – is attainable provided that citizens as tax-payers or funders of the system were prepared to pay more. Over and above any technical or physical constraints there may be on providing for expensive therapies, there is also a social choice about the appropriate level of healthcare a society should fund. Thus, decisions about whether to spend on certain interventions turns on a judgement of social values as to their relative priority compared with other forms of expenditure or more fecund forms of health expenditure. Whereas it might have been plausible, when the UN was drawing up its various declarations of rights, to suppose that the supply of medical care was somehow fixed by technical constraints, that assumption is no longer valid. What is necessarily involved is a judgement of relative social worth, and that is a distinct basis of judgement, conceptually, from the assertion of a right.

The right to health as the right to a fair share

Suppose we accept the argument to this point. That is to say, we can accept that a right to health can in some sense be regarded as the ground of provision for universal health services, but we also recognize that in dealing with issues of cost-effectiveness such services go beyond rights in the sense that we need to supplement the language of rights with the language of relative priorities. One inference that might be drawn is to say that justice in healthcare can be expressed in terms of the right to a fair share of resources in an institutionalized arrangement where there is collective burden-sharing and in which the principle of cost-effectiveness has a place. We move in effect from human rights to the rights of the political associate. In this way of thinking, the right to health becomes the conclusion of an argument rather than its premise. We design an institution to secure comprehensive, high-quality healthcare available without financial barriers to access, and within that structure we work out what a cost-effective level of provision will be. The right to health then becomes one's fair share of the benefits of this collective arrangement.

This way conceiving the right to health is not entirely at odds with a general human rights way of thinking, including that found in the existing UN human rights declarations and conventions. Thus, Article 20 of the 1951 Convention Relating to the Status of Refugees says: 'Where a rationing system exists, which applies to the population at large and regulates the distribution of products in short supply, refugees shall be accorded the same treatment as nationals.' A similar provision applies to housing, which is typically inelastic in supply and therefore has characteristics akin to those goods usually subject to rationing. According to this view of rights, where a scheme of rationing exists, it would be wrong to exclude refugees from participating on the same terms as other members of the population subject to a government, since otherwise their human rights would be breached. The rights claim functions in part in the form noted above, namely as a ground of inclusion relating to the idea of equality, but the content of the right is given by whatever shares are determined by the functioning system of rationing.

Rights discourse can even go beyond these considerations. Instead of simply saying that to have a right to health is to have a fair share in a scheme developed to mutual advantage, the idea of a right can also be used to help us understand what is involved in the definition of a fair share. To see how this might be so, we need to understand that although the approach of beneficial design might appear to favour a maximizing principle in respect of QALYs, this is not the only way in which the promotion of benefit might be understood. The idea of the right to health can block such maximizing logic.

A QALY is simply a measure of benefit. As such, it says nothing about how resources are to be directed or the principles upon which QALYs are to be promoted. However, one particular approach has been influential in discussions of public choice in respect of QALYs, namely that those responsible for allocating medical care resources should seek to maximize the number of QALYs they secure for any given level of expenditure. In other words, the claim is that a social optimum of expenditure balances the total expenditure incurred with the total benefit received. One way of arriving at this conclusion is as follows. If we use a QALY assessment to decide how to choose between two alternative interventions as to relative cost-effectiveness, then it would be rational to choose the more cost-effective of the two, thus maximizing the ratio of benefit to expenditure. If we now compare successive interventions, we would rationally favour the more effective of the two in each case, and we can go on making these comparisons until we end up with that set of interventions that a superior in cost-effectiveness terms to all others through a succession of pair-wise comparisons. This set will be those interventions that maximize the value of QALYs as a whole.

However, in response to this maximizing approach, there are some well-known objections, two of which two are particularly worth mentioning. The first is that the application of a simple aggregative rule of this sort will lead to situations in which a relatively small number of patients with severe conditions will secure less priority than a large number of patients with mild conditions. Although the QALY gain per person for the second group may not be large in itself, the maximization of benefit will lead to a preference for interventions to deal with the mild conditions because of the larger number of people who can benefit. As such, this would be contrary to the principle of sharing the financial costs of serious illness, costs that can reach a catastrophic scale. The second is that the estimate of any QALY gain is independent of the age at which it occurs. Yet, there are reasons for thinking that age is an important consideration, at least for life-threatening conditions that strike people at a relatively young age. This consideration is controversial among those who have discussed the issue, but in itself this is to say that one cannot just rest content with an assumption that a maximizing approach to QALYs is the right goal for a public healthcare system. (For these points, see, in a large literature: Battin 1987, Hadorn 1991, and Menzel 2006.)

These consequences are merely one example of a well-known tendency of maximizing decisions strategies deriving from a certain kind of utilitarianism to over-ride individual interests in ways that seem unfair. In this context, an attraction of rights discourse is its role in protecting the legitimate basic interests of individuals. As Jones (1994) puts it:

> Rights are what individuals are entitled to in and of themselves. Individuals should not be treated as mere means to be used in the pursuit of a social optimum and they should not be thought of as possessing rights only because and to the extent that their possession of these rights serves some general social purpose. The form in which this complaint has come to be stated is that utilitarianism ignores 'the separateness of persons .... (p. 62)

The claim that utilitarianism does not recognize the separateness of persons of course goes back to Rawls (1999, pp. 29–30). Rawls's own characterization of the contrast – that justice as fairness regards society as a scheme of cooperation for reciprocal advantage regulated by principles which persons would choose in an initial situation that is fair, whereas utilitarianism sees society as a problem of the efficient administration of social resources to maximize the satisfaction of the system of desire constructed by an impartial spectator – is often taken to be definitive. And if one takes utilitarianism to be the principle that aggregate utility (however defined) is to be maximized, then it is easy to see how a contrast in principle can be established. A beneficial design that merely aggregated individual utilities might easily end up ignoring the separateness of persons.

From this point of view, rights discourse grades human interests and levels of well-being in terms of their relative importance. To respect the rights' component of a health policy judgement is to acknowledge that some diseases are more important for public policy than others – for example, that life-saving therapies are more important than the relief of mild pain – and that the aggregation of small benefits for the many cannot justify imposition of severe deprivation on the few. If we think of the implications of this approach for practical decision making, then it affects the way in which cost-sharing arrangements are defined. Its logical corollary is to give priority to expensive but effective life-saving therapies over interventions where the costs of treatment can be borne by individuals and where the condition is not serious.

Conclusion

There are a number of roles the language of rights can play in defining the principles that would characterize a modern and civilized medical care system. The right to health can be seen as a ground justifying a modern medical care system, suitably expanded from its abstract formulation to a more developed account of what this right involves in practice. An appeal to rights also establishes claims to the standing of individuals within the scope of the benefits supplied by such a system, lying behind the specific features of an institutional design perspective. However, although the language of rights has these positive roles, it is less helpful when it comes to matters of adjudicating questions of cost-effectiveness. There is an irreducible element in any distinctive notion of a human right that marks the insistence on the absolute wrongness involved in treating people in certain ways. In practice, necessity may override the requirements of rights, but that is a different matter from saying that goods need to be fairly distributed as a matter of relative priority. Rights guard against the oppression of the misuse of political authority or the tyranny of the majority, but they form a less useful conceptual apparatus when considering how citizens might allocate entitlements among themselves in a social contract that is practically viable.

Although a health social contract goes beyond rights to questions of institutional design, we can still find elements of the values that use of rights language seeks to uphold. This is particularly so when we consider what would constitute the right to a fair share in a social contract for healthcare. Recognition of rights guards against a simple maximizing strategy to secure the basic interests that human have in living their lives well. The role of rights discourse is limited in this regard, since there are still serious issues of cost-effectiveness and relative priority even when the best has been done to secure basic interests. Nevertheless, insofar as rights also mark out claims of equality and inclusiveness, they help ensure that the social contract for health is one that fairly spreads the burdens and obligations of cost-effectiveness, summed up in the duty to accept that no life is literally 'beyond price' among political associates.

Throughout his work, Jones has always sought to scotch two competing errors typically associated with rights. The first is that all that is important in normative political theory is captured in the language of rights. The second is that nothing that is important in normative political theory is captured in the language of rights. In this paper I have sought to show that in the case of healthcare it ought to be possible to find a way 'between utility and rights' (Hart 1983). From this perspective, beneficial design need not be construed in terms of an institution that promotes a social goal specified in terms of aggregate utility. Rather a beneficial institutional design needs to be subject to the constraint that compared with some baseline of non-cooperation it is beneficial for all, or at least any, of the associates. In this way it would respect the separateness of persons, and thus capture what is important about rights, as well as to conform to the social values that would enable those same associates to assess its performance. Developing such a theory latent in a tradition requires much more work. But if the concerns of those who sought to establish the right to the highest attainable level of healthcare are to be taken seriously, then such a combination is needed in the construction of medical care systems, if that construction is also to provide a means by which beneficial institutional can be realized. That theory will be immeasurably aided by paying careful attention to the work of Peter Jones.

Acknowledgements

This is a revised version of a paper presented at the conference held in honour of Peter Jones, entitled 'The Value and Limits of Rights', at Newcastle University, Newcastle upon Tyne, 25–26 February 2010. I am grateful to the participants at the conference for discussion; and to Peter Jones and Sarah Clark for their comments; as well as to Michael Freeman who commented on a much earlier version of this paper. This paper forms part of my work under an Economic and Social Research Council (ESRC) Professorial Fellowship on 'Social Contract, Deliberative Democracy and Public Policy' (RES-051-27-0264).

References

Anscombe, E., 1967. But who is wronged? *Oxford Review*, 5, 16–17.
Backman, G., et al., 2008. The right to health. *Lancet*, 372, 2047–2085.
Battin, M.P., 1987. Age rationing and the just distribution of health care: is there a duty to die? *Ethics*, 97, 317–340.
Bellamy, R., 2012. Rights as democracy. *Critical Review of International Social and Political Philosophy*, 15 (4), 449–471.
Brownlie, I., 1981. *Basic documents on human rights*. 2nd edition. Oxford: Clarendon.
Dworkin, R., 1977. *Taking rights seriously*. London: Duckworth.
Dworkin, R., 2000. Justice and the high cost of health. *In*: R. Dworkin, ed. *Sovereign virtue*. Cambridge, MA: Harvard University Press, 307–319.

Freeman, M., 2009. The right to health. *In*: R. Morgan and R.S. Turner, eds. *Interpreting human rights: social science perspectives*. London: Routledge, 44–67.

Griffin, J., 2001. Discrepancies between the best philosophical account of human rights and the international law of human rights. *Proceedings of the Aristotelian Society*, n.s. 101, 1–28.

Hadorn, D.C., 1991. Setting health care priorities in Oregon: cost-effectiveness meets the rule of rescue. *Journal of the American Medical Association*, 265, 2218–2225.

Hart, H.L.A., 1983. Between utility and rights. *In*: H.L.A. Hart, ed. *Essays in jurisprudence and Philosophy*. Oxford: Clarendon, 198–222.

Jones, P., 1994. *Rights*. Houndmills: Macmillan.

Menzel, P., 2006. Allocation of scarce medical resources. *In*: R. Rhodes, L. Francis, and A. Silvers, eds. *Blackwell guide to medical ethics*. Oxford: Blackwell, 305–322.

National Institute for Health and Clinical Excellence (NICE), 2008. *Social value judgements*. Available from: http://www.nice.org.uk/media/C18/30/SVJ2PUBLICATION2008.pdf/.

Nozick, R., 1974. *Anarchy, state and utopia*. Oxford: Basil Blackwell.

O'Neill, O., 2002. Public health or clinical ethics: thinking beyond borders. *Ethics and International Affairs*, 16, 35–45.

Rawls, J., 1999. *A theory of justice*. Revd edition. Oxford: Oxford University Press.

Raz, J., 1986. *The morality of freedom*. Oxford: Clarendon Press.

Raz, J., 1990. *Practical reason and norms*. Princeton, NJ: Princeton University Press.

Rueda, P., 2010. Legal language and social change during Colombia's economic crisis. *In*: J. Couso, A. Huneeus, and R. Sieder, eds. *Cultures of legality*. New York, NY: Cambridge University Press, 25–50.

Sikora, K., 2007. Insurance policy promises to supply the drugs NHS will not pay for. *The Times*, 25 April.

Steiner, H., 1994. *An essay on rights*. Oxford: Blackwell.

Weale, A., 1998. Editorial: Rationing health care: a logical solution to an inconsistent triad. *British Medical Journal, no.*, 7129 (7), 410.

White, J., 1995. *Competing solutions: American health care proposals and international experience*. Washington, DC: The Brookings Institution.

Wolff, J., 2012. The demands of the human right to health. *Proceedings of the Aristotelian Society*, 86 (1), 217–237.

The value and limits of rights: a reply

Peter Jones

School of Geography, Politics & Sociology, Newcastle University, Newcastle upon Tyne, UK

> I reply to each of the contributions in this issue. I agree with much that Hillel Steiner argues, especially his insistence that the associated ideas of impartiality and discontinuity are crucial to dealing satisfactorily with a diversity of competing claims. I am, however, less willing to conceive provision for that diversity as *the* role, rather than *a* role, that we should ascribe to rights. I question the success of David Miller's endeavour to provide a unified justification of human rights grounded in the concept of need. It is the notion of a minimally decent human life, rather than need itself, that does most of the justificatory work in Miller's argument and, arguably, that notion does not deliver a genuinely unitary account of human rights. I concede the case for state funding of opera and the arts more generally to John Horton's argument, but defend neutralism, and its associated distinction between the right and the good, as a strategy for dealing with diversity, including cultural diversity. I resist Richard Bellamy's attempt to ground all basic rights in democracy and suggest that his argument relies upon idealized assumptions about the functioning of democracy. I share much of his objection to substituting judicial for political decision-making but argue that a strong moral commitment to rights need not imply a shift in power from democratic processes to courts. I endorse Albert Weale's argument for favouring a beneficial design approach over a rights approach to healthcare and to many other social goods. Rights should not monopolize our moral and political thinking.

I am greatly honoured that a group of such distinguished scholars should have been willing to give their attention to my research. I am also most grateful to Ian O'Flynn and Albert Weale for organizing the conference at which these papers were first presented and for editing this special issue of the journal. To receive the critical attention of so many famous names in British political philosophy is a rare luxury. This collection has a special value for me since the contributors have been friends and colleagues throughout my academic career and I have gained immeasurably from the intellectual life that I have shared with them over several decades. Our thinking on common concerns has sometimes converged and often differed, but all of the contributors have had a major impact on my own thinking and the debt I owe them extends far beyond this collection.

While the experience of having one's work scrutinized by such an able body of scholars is both gratifying and flattering, it is also humbling and chastening. I find myself called to account for unguarded comments and breezy generalizations that I managed to slip past editors and journal referees many years ago. I cannot make the usual excuse of youthful excess, since most of my indiscretions belong to middle age and sometimes quite late middle age. That said, I am chastened only to a limited degree and in limited respects. Perhaps unwisely, I remain stubbornly attached to most of the positions to which I committed my former self and the stubbornness with which I defend and reassert those positions will be more apparent in what follows than my readiness to learn from criticism. The Socratic nature of analytical political philosophy pushes its practitioners towards disputation; too much agreement would threaten the subject's survival. But persuasion and progress in understanding are possible even in political philosophy and I have found much to learn from and to assent to in the papers that make up this collection. I need hardly say that the brief responses I give to them in this Reply will not do justice to the subtle and detailed arguments they contain, particularly since those arguments often grow out of much larger bodies of work for which their authors have become well known and justly celebrated.

Disagreement, discontinuity and rights

In the 1980s Robert Goodin and Andrew Reeve invited me to write an essay on the neutral state for their volume entitled *Liberal Neutrality* (1989). Writing that essay was something of a Damascene experience and very much of what I have written since has had its origins in issues the essay made me confront. Like many contemporary political theorists, I have been preoccupied with the diversity that characterizes the populations of modern societies and with the question of how a population should provide for its own diversity. More particularly, I have been concerned with the differences of belief, value and culture, because those differences present us not merely with 'difference' but with conflict. In that context, it is easy to see the appeal of a neutralist strategy: if an arrangement providing for conflicting beliefs and values is to be *acceptable* to people, and if they are to accept it as *fair*, it cannot be one that simply privileges and imposes a belief or value that is part of the very conflict for which it aims to provide. It has to be an arrangement that is grounded independently of the beliefs and values at issue and which, in that sense, deals with the conflict neutrally. It should regulate the conflict without becoming party to it.

Hillel Steiner has obviously felt the appeal of this approach every bit as strongly as I have. His own defence of the case for a neutral or impartial strategy in the face of conflicting beliefs and values has been eloquent, both here and elsewhere. Steiner makes sparing use of the language of 'neutrality' and it is perhaps unfortunate that the strategy to which we both subscribe should have been characterized primarily in those terms, since it has occasioned much misplaced criticism. For instance, critics have complained that it is impossible to be neutral about everything, but no neutralist has ever said otherwise. In particular, neutralists are not neutral about the principles that inform or ground their neutralism; but it does not follow that there is no credible sense in which their approach is authentically neutral in the way it deals with the diversity for which it is designed. The relevant strategy can be and has been characterized in other terms, particularly the distinction between the 'right' and the 'good'. Like Steiner, my own preferred characterization is the distinction between 'discontinuous' and 'continuous' strategies for dealing with diversity, a distinction due to Ronald Dworkin (Dworkin 1990, pp. 16–22). Neutralism belongs in the discontinuous stable, since it aims to establish a discontinuity between the diversity at stake and the principles that are used to regulate it. A continuous strategy, by contrast, seeks a solution based on values that are somehow continuous with those that are in conflict and for which it has to provide.

There are many cases in which a continuous strategy is not feasible. Take the case of religious differences. If a population tries to provide political arrangements that deal fairly with differences in religious faith, an approach that searches for a solution in the very beliefs that are in conflict is decidedly unpromising. Much more promising is an approach that requires the parties to step outside their religious bunkers and to see themselves not as adherents of this or that religion but as people who hold different and conflicting religious beliefs. They should then think about what would be a fair arrangement amongst people so circumstanced. Nowadays, the religious are likely to protest that their faiths are intrinsically tolerant and contain within themselves the solution to the diversity they present; in other words, there can be a continuity between different and conflicting faiths and the values that we call upon to provide for that difference. However, viewed historically, it is hard to find that claim convincing. If the political values of freedom and equality were written into Christianity and Islam all along, it is surprising that it took so long for their sponsors to discover them. Much more plausible is the story that John Rawls tells – a story of faiths gradually adjusting and amending their doctrines to remove dissonances between their doctrine and changed moral and political thinking on liberty and equality. The slow and reluctant way in which the Roman Catholic Church came to accept democracy and human rights is a perfect example of this process of gradual adjustment (Curran 1998). It may be plausibly claimed, as Rawls does, that an overlapping consensus amongst religions on acceptable political arrangements now exists in many liberal societies, but that is not a consensus that was there all along. Nor is it one formed around principles of liberty and equality and political practices and institutions that owe their origin only to religious doctrine.

My own thinking on these issues has been heavily influenced by Rawls even though, like many of his fellow travellers, I have sometimes bitten the hand that has fed me. The strategy of discontinuity is not unique to Rawls, and it was a strategy he thought appropriate only to a society characterized by pluralism and a liberal democratic political culture (Rawls 1993, 1999). Steiner's commitment to the idea of, and need for, discontinuity is not similarly circumscribed nor, as far as I can see, is it similarly indebted to Rawls. Unlike most of the major political theories that have been developed in recent decades, Steiner's work, especially his *An Essay on Rights* (1994), is distinguished by its lack of indebtedness to Rawls, even as an adversary.

How then does discontinuity relate to the purpose and content of rights? For Steiner, it is disagreement and the need to provide for it discontinuously that explains both the purpose of rights and the moral priority they enjoy. These also intimate what it is that rights must be rights to: domains within which the right-holder alone is free to determine what shall be done. By comparison with the simple austerity of Steiner's view, my more varied conception of the purpose and content of rights will appear decidedly promiscuous. However, I certainly agree with Steiner in giving disagreement and diversity a major role in determining the purpose and content of rights. Rights have to make sense in, and have to provide for, a world in which people hold different beliefs, values and commitments. Those rights include human rights and the differences they have to address include cultural differences.

David Miller detects a difference in emphasis between my approach in *Rights* (1994) and in articles on rights that I wrote thereafter, a difference, he suggests, that is to be explained by my having discovered 'culture'. I have indeed argued that, in conformity with the strategy of discontinuity, we might conceive human rights as standing in a second-order and regulative relation to cultural differences (Jones 2001). That argument does presuppose that cultural difference deserves to be taken seriously, but it does not entail that our response to cultures must be indiscriminate. It also leaves human rights in a position of moral primacy. I remain resistant to the way in which 'culture' is frequently deployed as a trump card in contemporary political argument and wary of attempts to sanctify practices and shield them from critical discussion by branding them 'cultural'. One reason for my taking up the issue of how human rights relate to cultural diversity was the common complaint (more common nowadays than in 1948) that the doctrine of human rights imposes a particular form of life – Western and liberal – upon humanity at large. Human rights advocates now find themselves caricatured as marauding imperialists callously trying to stop practices such as torture and tyrannously imposing freedom of thought and freedom of religion upon populations. For some Western critics, it would seem that non-Western populations, in embracing human rights, are merely running headlong to their chains. Protests about the alien influence of human rights and liberalism are rarely accompanied by similar protests against the influence of ideologies such as nationalism and Marxism, which are every bit as 'Western' in origin and which often play a significant role in 'non-Western' violations of human rights.

In fact, the generality of human rights, that now figure in a plethora of international declarations, covenants and conventions, do very little to impose a specific form of life on populations. On the whole they establish a framework intended to give people the freedom and opportunity to live whatever form of life they wish or believe to be right, including the most communal of communitarian forms of life. In Miller's own terms, they aim to secure the conditions for a minimally decent human life without specifying in any detail what particular life that should be. Insofar as a diversity of beliefs, wishes and aspirations is part of the world for which human rights have to provide, those rights can, should and often do, take account of that diversity. They do not, of course, sanction every kind of practice; they would be pointless if they did. But, in the jargon of neutralism, they seek to lay down certain rules of right within which people are able and free to pursue different conceptions of the good.

In arguing that the theory of human rights needed to take cultural diversity seriously, I did not mean to suggest that that was the sole or main purpose of human rights. As I have already indicated, my efforts to link the role of rights to the facts of pluralism and disagreement have been more modest and qualified than Steiner's. My view has been that the purpose that has done most to prompt the ideas of natural and human rights has been the protection of people from abuses of power, particularly political power. Rights, such as rights to freedom of thought, conscience and religion and rights not to suffer certain forms of discrimination, clearly do provide for differences, while rights not to be tortured, to be tried fairly, and not to suffer cruel, inhuman and degrading treatment, have a purpose that lies elsewhere. But even those commonly claimed human rights that relate less immediately to diversity, such as those I have just cited, along with rights relating to judicial processes, personal security and basic socioeconomic goods, remain consistent with a multitude of different forms of life.

Grounding human rights

The diverse content of human rights has led me to think that the justification of human rights might also need to be diverse. In proposing a pluralistic approach to the justification of human rights, I do not mean to suggest that all of the various extant justificatory theories of human rights could contribute to the task. As Miller points out, that could not make sense since those theories are frequently incompatible. Rather my thought has been the more modest one that different rights may be rights for different reasons, and that the reasons that justify different rights can be different without being incompatible. I mean to cast doubt on the assumption, widely shared amongst who take on the daunting task of justifying human rights, that all of these rights can stem, or should stem, from a single justificatory root.

Miller resists this doubt and remains committed to a unified justification of human rights. He has long been a proponent of need as a normative notion that should contribute to our thinking on justice and he is joined by many others, including myself, in holding that need should contribute to our thinking on human rights. However, needs have been most frequently invoked in relation to socio-economic human rights; Miller is unusual in proposing that need can ground every sort of human right.

I remain sceptical about Miller's bold claim in a number of ways, all of which concern the way in which he links need to the idea of a minimally decent human life (MDHL). First, he does not claim that need alone can do the job; rather, it is need in conjunction with the notion of a MDHL. That gives us reason to suspect that the primary normative work is being done by the notion of a MDHL rather than by the notion of need. Once we have established, or have taken for granted, that everyone is entitled to a MDHL, we can go on to argue that everyone is also entitled to whatever he or she needs to live a MDHL. (That is not quite true because, there may be elements of MDHL to which we do not think people have rights, e.g. love and friendship.) But what gives moral force to claims of need and what gives content to those claims will be our notion of a MDHL.

Secondly, we may question whether the idea of MDHL provides a genuinely monistic justification of human rights. T. M. Scanlon has argued that we should not think of well-being as a 'master value' (Scanlon 1998, pp. 108–143); it is not 'a good separate from other values, which are made valuable in turn by the degree to which they promote it' (p. 142). It is better understood as an 'inclusive good': one that encompasses the various particular goods that contribute to a life's going well. That would seem even more clearly true of a MDHL; that life is not a good in its own right from which all of the things that contribute to it derive their value. It is a portmanteau term that we use to encompass all of the various things that make up a life's being 'decent'. If that is so, we can still think about human rights in terms of needs but the meeting of those needs will not promote a single unitary goal that we can label a MDHL. Rather it will provide for the many and various constituents of a MDHL. In other words, our ability to appeal to the idea of MDHL in justifying human rights does not suffice to show that that justification will be genuinely monistic in character.

Thirdly, in speaking of what is needed for a MDHL, there is a risk of conflating the *instruments* necessary for attaining a MDHL and the essential *constituents* of a MDHL. Miller seems to stick consistently to an instrumental notion of need and I do not suggest therefore that he is guilty of this conflation when he argues that all human rights can be understood as catering for what is needed for a MDHL. However, the claim that all human rights answer to needs is certainly more plausible if need is ambiguous between instruments and constituents. For example, if we say that the right to a fair trial (which we may generalize as a right to be treated fairly by the judicial system to which one is subject) is needed for a MDHL, that is much more persuasive if we think of the possession of that right as itself part of – as itself a constituent of – a MDHL. It is much less persuasive if we have to view the right to a fair trial as an instrument of – as something that provides a resource for – the attainment of a MDHL. We can certainly tell a story about how the fairness of trials might serve other goods that matter to people, but that is not the whole story nor are we likely to regard it as the most important story we should tell if we were asked to defend the human right to a fair trial. We are much more likely to think that being tried unfairly is, of itself, an injustice and, for that reason, the violation of a human right, irrespective of whatever other ills the victim suffers as a consequence of his unfair treatment.

It is, of course, much easier to pick holes in someone else's justification of human rights than oneself to come up with an alternative that will do better. Even if we do opt for a pluralistic approach, the task is still daunting. But I want to pray in aid here an observation that I previously made on human rights and one to which Miller refers: the observation that 'the traditional political purpose of natural or human rights has been to tell those who wield political power what they may and may not do' (Jones 1994, p. 222).[1] If that is true – and I still think it is – we should, in cataloguing human rights, be particularly aware of the respects in which people might be mistreated by political power and therefore of the different sorts of safeguard they will need. If we approach the compilation of a catalogue of human rights with that purpose in mind, it will be unsurprising if the human rights we end up with are a rather heterogeneous set – such as, for example, the rights to security of person, freedom of religion, social security, a nationality, and a fair trial (all of which appear in the United Nations' Universal Declaration of Human Rights (UDHR) 1948). We might speak of all of these rights as rights that people 'need' to secure them from the abuse of power, but that does not indicate that need contributes significantly to the reasons for these rights being rights.

I do, however, want to add a comment on that approach. While I think providing safeguards and guarantees in relation to political power has been the principal driving concern behind the natural and human rights tradition, I do not mean that to be definitive of human rights. Some authors have defined human rights as rights only against governments (e.g. Martin 1993). By contrast, I would see taming political power as one of the major – and as historically perhaps the major – practical implication of ascribing rights to human beings as human beings. But the idea of human rights is not, and should not be, limited to that domain. If, for example, an individual is abused by a commercial organization in the same way as he might have been abused by a government, and if that abuse by a government would have been the violation of a human right, I see no good reason for denying that the commercial organization violates a human right. Similarly, if the idea of human rights brings with it an idea of the fundamentally equal moral status amongst human beings, I see no reason why human rights might not be invoked when we condemn the unequal treatment of women. So, although I think that human rights have been conceived primarily in relation to governments and although the provision of safeguards against political power can help to make sense of the heterogeneity of human rights, I do not suggest that the very idea of a human right should be confused with that purpose.

Neutrality, the right and the good

If my thinking about rights has been more modestly 'discontinuous' than Steiner's and if it has verged on being too discontinuous to satisfy Miller, its having aspired to discontinuity in any measure has been enough to earn the scepticism of John Horton. He is sceptical of the entire family of neutralist or impartialist forms of liberalism, and their efforts to distinguish the right from the good. He takes me to task for commenting that 'the real test of a liberal is whether one believes that it is permissible for the state to subsidise opera'. While I cannot now recall saying that, I do not doubt that I did. I hope I said it ironically and with a smile on my face, but I cannot be sure that I was not in earnest.[2] Certainly if we do adopt a distinction between the right and the good and require political power to concern itself with nothing but the right, we would seem to remove state patronage of the arts and much else besides from the political agenda. Some liberals have tried to make a case for state funding of the arts that avoids any claim that they are of intrinsic worth but, like Horton, I find their efforts desperate and unconvincing. In truth, I do not want to embargo the state's supporting opera, or other art forms, or museums and libraries. As Horton acknowledges, there is a legitimate argument to be had about state subsidies for opera and the case for those subsidies has to be made. He rightly mocks the idea that anyone is 'disrespected' if their state supports opera, but the more pertinent Rawlsian question is whether that support is fair. Is it fair that public funds should be used to support a form of entertainment that is enjoyed by only a minority of taxpayers, most of whom come from the better-off section of society, particularly if there is no counterbalancing use of taxpayers' money to support other, more 'popular', forms of entertainment? The fact that the sum of money involved is paltry compared with other government expenditure does not dispose of the issue of principle. If a satisfactory justification is to be found, it cannot be one that claims that some people – those with a taste for opera – should count for more than others. It must be more impersonal in form: opera has an intrinsic worth that merits public support. On that point, as on so much else, I agree with Brian Barry (Barry 2001, pp. 198–199). State subsidy of opera is likely to escape the charge of unfairness only if it is conceived as not a matter of fairness at all.

However, while I am willing to run up the white flag in the case of opera, I am not similarly willing to renounce my use of the distinction between the right and the good in other contexts. Apart from the case of opera, Horton focuses his critique of that distinction mainly upon my use of it in relation to cultural diversity. I was aware that applying the distinction to cultural differences was particularly provocative, since a culture is often thought to be something that we cannot get 'outside' and view impartiality. Even so, it is commonplace for people to insist that in a multicultural society, cultural differences should be provided for justly or fairly or equally. That, in turn, implies that a society should, in its public life, be impartial in its treatment of the cultural differences present in its population.[3] It is not unusual to hear people insist that this sort of impartiality is impossible, but then go on to complain bitterly about partiality or bias a society displays in its treatment of different cultures. I do not claim that it is practically possible or even desirable for a society to be impartial with respect to everything that the sprawling term 'culture' might encompass. Language is often cited as an example of something on which it is neither practicable not desirable that a society should be neutral, although some societies, like Belgium and Canada, do endeavour to be even-handed between two languages. But if we accept that a society cannot be, or should not be, impartial about *everything*, it does not follow that it cannot be, or should not be, impartial about *anything*. The shift in perspective that I cited earlier in relation to religious difference can also be made in relation to cultural difference. That is we, as the members of a multicultural society, rather than seeing the world and making demands only from the blinkered perspective of our own culture, can shift to a perspective in which we see ourselves and our fellow citizens as possessors of different cultural inheritances and commitments. We can also appreciate that other's inheritances and commitments matter to them as ours do to us. We can then begin to think about what constitutes a fair arrangement amongst citizens who possess different cultural allegiances.

This shift in perspective is sometimes said to be impossible and to require people to be schizophrenic. But that is melodramatic nonsense. It is a shift that we very commonly make. That is, rather than living in a solipsistic bubble in which we are sensitive to nothing but our own preferences and commitments, we are normally aware that others have preferences and commitments that differ from our own. There is nothing unusual or farfetched in our then seeing ourselves as one person amongst many, each of whom is of equal status, and going on to think about what would be the right or the fair arrangement when we see the world in that way. That, for instance, was the perspective adopted by Rowan Williams as Archbishop of Canterbury when he called for the protection afforded to Christianity by the English common law of blasphemy to be extended to Islam and other non-Christian faiths.

That shift in perspective alone is not guaranteed to deliver unanimity on what constitutes the fair treatment of differences. The distinction between the right and the good sometimes goes along with the claim that those who possess different and conflicting conceptions of the good can nevertheless agree upon the principles of right that should regulate their pursuit of those conceptions. That claim is sometimes justified. For instance, in most liberal democratic societies there is a broad consensus upon the principle of freedom of religion and one that includes those who possess different religious beliefs. There are sometimes, of course, disputes about how precisely that principle should be translated into public policy, but those disputes arise within a consensus on the general principle of freedom of religion. However, I do not claim that issues of right will always be free of controversy, but, even if they are not, that is no reason to rubbish the distinction between the right and the good, since the distinction marks a difference of kind between issues. Argument about the correct or best conception of the good and argument about the right principles for regulating relations amongst people who have different and conflicting conceptions of the good, are arguments about different sorts of issue. Plato notwithstanding, I cannot see why all of our moral thinking should be reducible, without loss, to an undifferentiated moral blob that we label 'the good'.

The case of *cultural* difference is particularly challenging because of the all-enveloping content that we commonly give that concept, but the shift in perspective I describe would still be possible and significant if, as Horton alleges, cultures penetrate the right. We can still distinguish between the role and status of principles conceived merely as the principles of a particular culture from principles designed to provide fairly for differences amongst cultures. There is one respect in which I still want to resist the sort of ultimacy that Horton claims for 'culture'. My argument has been that insofar as cultures matter, they matter primarily if and because they matter to those who bear them. Thus, our ultimate concern should be not for cultures but for those whose cultures they are. I still think it no less bizarre to ascribe moral standing to a culture qua culture than to a painting or a musical composition or a language (Jones 1998, p. 36). If I am correct about that, the issue at the level of the right should be about which people should count and about what follows from their counting; it will not be about which culture qua culture we should knuckle under. Nor, if cultures incorporate principles of the right, can we burke this issue by leaving it to be determined by each culture since, logically, the issue of moral standing, and who possesses it, must precede claims of culture.

Horton expresses some surprise that I allow that impartial arrangements need not be liberal arrangements. If we believe that the ultimate units of standing should be individuals, it is still open to people to argue that some individuals should count for more than others. While I, of course, sympathize with Steiner's claim that human individuals should enjoy an equality of status, I am less sanguine than he is of the ease with which its triumph will be secured, although we can reasonably place the onus of justification upon those who wish to depart from equality. Groups rather than individuals might also be proposed as the relevant units of standing. Another option is resort to a procedural rather than a substantive form of impartiality. For example, a society might deal with cultural difference by way of democracy and majority rule, so that the culture that shapes a society's public life is whatever culture a majority of its members votes for. We may regard the outcome of that procedure as substantively unfair, but a procedure can be fair qua procedure even though it yields an unfair outcome. A commitment to democracy together with majority rule can count as an authentic commitment to impartiality, provided that it is a principled commitment to the fairness of the procedure and not a commitment contingent upon a particular outcome. A group cannot claim to be authentically committed to procedural impartiality if it demands equal rights when it is in the minority and unequal rights when it is in the majority. Most of the critical comment upon neutralism or impartiality has focused upon whether it is possible. The burden of my argument here and elsewhere is that more of it should be about whether neutrality or impartiality is justified and, if so, what form it should take, and how extensive its range should be.

While Horton is generally sceptical of the whole neutralist approach, and particularly of the distinction between the right and the good, much of his argument is directed not at the discontinuous strategy as such but at its 'misguidedly rigorist' forms. I have no wish to defend 'rigorism'. Being committed to a principle does not mean that we have to be fanatical and unyielding in our commitment and bone-headedly oblivious to other considerations. Nor does it compel us to ignore the fact that we start not with a blank sheet but with a particular society and a particular historical legacy. Horton cites the case of the established Church of England as an example of non-neutral arrangement that does not evoke complaints of unfairness and unequal respect from other Christian denominations or other faiths.

Like Barry (again), I am phlegmatic about the established status of the Church of England (Barry 1995, p. 165). The reality in Britain is that neither other variants of Christianity, nor non-Christian faiths, nor even secularism, are significantly disadvantaged by church establishment in its contemporary form. Horton rightly notices that the adherents of other faiths now sometimes given their blessing to the established church, but that is because they have come to regard secularism, rather than one another, as their principal enemy. In their eyes, disestablishment would be a victory for secularism rather than a blow for religious equality. However, in the different world of 19th-century Britain, when Anglicanism really was privileged, dissenting Protestants objected very strongly to establishment and sought its abolition. Moreover, if we really could scrape the canvas clean and start afresh, it is hard to imagine anyone, including Anglicans, pressing the case for an established church.

Rights and democracy

Horton's opposition to distinguishing the right from the good is matched by Richard Bellamy's opposition to separating rights from democracy. Both see giving a distinct and privileged status to rights and 'the right' as part of a misguided attempt to take them 'out of politics'. Bellamy challenges any suggestion, including my own, that rights might properly function as constraints upon democratic politics.

We might distinguish between two categories of right: those that we conceive as 'human' or 'fundamental' rights and those of a more quotidian and prosaic sort. We generally give the former, but not the latter, a special political status and one reason for that, I have argued, is because we believe they should serve as checks on political power. I take it that, while Bellamy may be concerned with both sorts of right, he also has particularly in mind rights of the former sort – rights of particular moment, such as the right to be tried fairly or the right not to be tortured. However, he argues that it is a mistake to conceive these rights as checks upon political power, or at least as checks upon democratic power. Rather than pit rights against democracy, we should think of rights as the offspring of democracy. We should place rights 'inside' rather than 'outside' democratic politics. Bellamy accepts another distinction that I make: that between 'democratic rights' (rights that are intrinsic to the democratic process, such as the rights to vote and to freedom of expression) and 'non-democratic rights' (rights that are concerned with something other than the democratic process, such as rights to freedom of religion, to be tried fairly, and not to be subjected to torture). But he argues that rights of both sorts are properly grounded in democracy and, in that respect, both might be described as 'democratic rights'.

Bellamy's argument relates (1) to the way we should think of the rights that people have and (2) to the institutions that we should employ to uphold and safeguard those rights. For Bellamy, these two issues are closely related but here I want to address them separately. How then should we think of having rights? In virtue of what can people claim rights? Bellamy's answer is: as the citizens of a democratic society. But how exactly are those citizens' rights grounded in democracy?

Parts of Bellamy's argument suggest a simple answer. In a democratic society, the demos possesses ultimate political authority on all matters, so that the members of that society will have all and only those rights that the demos decides they should have. We might describe this as the Hobbesian conception of democracy since it conceives the demos as 'sovereign' (in Hobbes's sense): for political purposes, the demos is the ultimate authority on all matters of right. One thing that suggests this understanding of Bellamy's argument is the stress he places on the extent and depth of disagreement that surrounds rights. The more we stress the inevitability and the inescapability of that disagreement, the more we are pushed towards a Hobbesian way of dealing with it. If this is how we should conceive the relationship between democracy and rights, we can do little more than sit back and let democracy takes its course: we will know what rights people have only once the democratic process has declared what rights they shall have. We may be able to anticipate what some of those rights will be, but they will actually be rights only if and when they receive the stamp of democratic authority.

Something that reinforces this understanding of Bellamy's position is his insistence that the democracy in which he grounds rights is not an idealized decision-procedure, analogous to those employed by Habermas and Rawls. Rather he means to ground rights in, and to derive them from, real-world democratic processes (pp. 451–452, 461). Yet, in spite of his protests to the contrary, there does seem to be an element of idealizing in Bellamy's argument. He commends us to think about rights in a 'democratic spirit' (pp. 451, 464) and to use 'democratic forms of reasoning' (p. 469). All rights, he says, 'involve a democratic form of justification – they imply a spirit of political equality to be accorded equal concern and respect' (p. 455). Political equality is, of course, fundamental to a democratic political system, but Bellamy seems to contemplate its being carried forward and instantiated in the decisions that the demos goes on to make. He makes clear that the democracy he contemplates is majoritarian democracy (p. 454), but he entertains none of the traditional fears for the fate of minorities. His lack of concern seems to derive from an assumption that his democratic citizens will always be good egalitarian citizens, who will treat people equally in the decisions they make as well as in the way they make them, and who will always pursue a good that is authentically public (pp. 458–459).

We may suspect that it is the principle of equal concern and respect, rather than democracy itself, that really drives Bellamy's argument. That principle would seem to justify both democratic decision-making and a set of rights. So, we might object, it is not democracy that grounds rights; rather the principle that justifies democracy also justifies rights, and it justifies rights not 'through', but independently of, democracy, so that those rights stand alongside democracy as its moral equals rather than its moral subordinates. However, Bellamy fends off that objection by arguing that we respect people equally only 'if their views have been equally considered' and we show them equal concern only 'through collective arrangements that can be shown to track their common recognisable interests' (p. 451; also pp. 454–455). In other words, equal concern and respect requires us to arrive at rights through a democratic process; if we take any other route to rights, we shall violate the principle of equal concern and respect and perhaps also the ideal 'non-domination'.

But, as I have already indicated, Bellamy's argument seems to suppose that the principle of equal concern and respect will shape not only political institutions and procedures but also the thoughts of democratic citizens as they enter the decision-making arena. Only if that is so, can we expect them to arrive at the rights that everyone ought to enjoy. If they fail to keep faith with that principle, they will fail to deliver the rights they should. It is in that respect that Bellamy's argument on rights strikes me as an exercise in ideal theory. It is an argument that contemplates the rights that people would settle on if they were deciding under genuinely democratic circumstances and with full respect for democratic principles.

There is another respect in which Bellamy's argument seems to belong to ideal theory. If rights are grounded in democracy and must be delivered by democracy, what are we to say of people who have the misfortune to live under undemocratic forms of government or in flawed democracies? Do they not have rights too? Bellamy recognizes this issue and sees the solution as the incorporation of the excluded into the democratic community where they will enjoy rights on equal terms with others (p. 460). But that does not tell us what rights people possess while they remain subject to the non-ideal circumstances of undemocratic government. These are precisely the circumstances in which we want to appeal to human rights – rights that people have in virtue of being human and that are violated by show-trials, genocidal campaigns, religious persecution, and the like. Any understanding of fundamental rights that precludes our saying that the Nazis or the Khmer Rouge violated rights is seriously hobbled and will not come anywhere close to playing the role that the conception of human rights has traditionally played.

My own approach to basic rights has been to ask what rights we have reason to attribute to people either as human beings or as citizens. The reasons will be moral reasons, but moral reasons informed by a knowledge of human beings and of human circumstances, including the realities of the political world and of political power. I think of those rights as moral rights, but as moral rights that have political implications; that is the only respect in which I will own up to thinking of rights as 'prior to politics'. I accept that a good argument is not enough to justify the imposition of a rights regime upon a population. Some sort of process of acceptance, either national or global, will be necessary to legitimate the regime, but legitimating the regime is not the same as, nor can it be a substitute for, working out what its content should be. In particular, when people enter the democratic arena, their acceptance that their decision should be made democratically will not tell them what their decision ought to be. They will necessarily invoke moral principles and considerations other than democracy, along with their knowledge of human circumstances and their beliefs about human interests. When moral and political philosophers argue about human rights, that is the sort of exercise in which I understand them to be engaged. Bellamy's claim seems to be not merely that a regime of rights must be endorsed by the population whose lives it will regulate, but also that the very idea of democracy and the very existence of a democratic process will somehow suffice to tell citizens what rights there ought to be. I cannot find that claim plausible, assuming that Bellamy expects democracy to deliver rights that will be similar in scope and substance to those enumerated in the United Nations' UDHR (1948) and not a severely attenuated set of rights relating only to political procedures.

When we shift from the question of what rights there should be to the issue of who should look after them, I can rival Bellamy in my reservations about constitutional entrenchment and judicial review. For example, I believe it little short of a scandal that a document, worded so generally and vaguely as the European Convention on Human Rights, should be administered by courts in the same way that they administer ordinary Parliamentary legislation. I do not blame the courts for this state of affairs. Judges are simply performing a task that the politicians have assigned them, and politicians' complaints about judicial decisions on, for example, privacy law often ring hollow because those same politicians are reluctant to grasp the nettle themselves and give courts clearer direction. My ideal state of affairs would be one in which the idea of human rights is heavily ingrained in a society's political culture, but one in which the conflicts of value and competing considerations that will inevitably arise in implementing rights are dealt with by democratic politicians in a good faith manner rather than by judges. As Bellamy quotes my saying, 'rights should be special, but their specialness should be felt in the way they are handled by politicians rather than in their not being handled by politicians' (Jones 1994, p. 225). So I have some sympathy with Bellamy's stance on these issues. However, his stance does raise questions relating to his own ideal of non-domination.

For the republican (e.g. Pettit 1997), there is a critical difference between not being interfered with and not being liable to interference. Even if I am liable to interference by another, I may not actually be interfered with and to that extent I may remain free. But my freedom will fall short of non-domination because I remain prey to the arbitrary interference of another. For republicans, freedom is a condition rather than a non-event; it consists in not being *liable* to interference by others. Now consider the conception of democracy that Bellamy offers us. That will be a democracy whose authority is in no way fettered by rights. But the existence of that comprehensive and unconstrained authority must mean that each individual citizen remains comprehensively at the mercy of the democratic sovereign and is therefore 'dominated' by it. Each citizen will of course have an equal vote with others in the exercise of that sovereignty, but for one individual amongst a demos numbered in millions that may offer little comfort. How could citizens become less dominated? The obvious answer is by acquiring constitutionally entrenched rights that limit the scope of democratic authority and that correspondingly enhance the non-dominance that each citizen enjoys. Each entrenched right would constitute an 'immunity', in relation to which others, including democratic governments, would possess a corresponding Hohfeldian 'disability' or 'no-power'. Each immunity would therefore be a zone of non-dominance. It would seem then that, contrary to the general thrust of Bellamy's argument, pursuit of non-dominance should lead us in the direction of constitutionally entrenched rights US style.

Bellamy seeks to resist that implication by talking up the potentially arbitrary, biased, elitist, controversial, and politically motivated nature of judicial decisions that rule on rights. But, while I share some of his worries about judicial discretion, being subject to the reasoning of a judge may still seem less arbitrary than being subject to the will of a legislature. Bellamy also seeks to fend off worries about unfettered democracy by stressing that democracy secures non-domination through its procedural features, rather than through the substance of its decisions. Perhaps that should lead us to voice a different worry: are the demands of non-domination being scaled back to secure a harmony between procedural democracy in general and its real world versions in particular?[4]

Bellamy associates my approach to rights with liberalism and with freedom conceived as non-interference, as distinct from the republican conception of non-domination. That is not an association, or dissociation, I recognize. Rights work differently from freedom. Republicans distinguish (what they reckon to be) the liberal conception of freedom as non-interference from their own conception of freedom as non-domination. However, it is hard to see how there might be two conceptions of rights that mimic those two conceptions of freedom. The idea of a right that one has only insofar as it remains uninfringed makes little sense. If we think merely in terms of liberty rights (what Hohfeld called 'privileges' and other sometimes call 'liberties' – the absence of obligations to the contrary), we could perhaps say that people have those rights insofar as they find themselves without obligations to the contrary and even though they may be liable to obligations to the contrary (e.g. by the creation of new obligations through legislation). But to present that as the 'liberal' conception of rights would be a travesty (and no less of a travesty just because Hobbes – a favourite 'liberal' of the republicans – understood natural rights as liberty rights). For liberals, as for others, significant rights, such as human rights or the rights of citizens, are claim-rights or immunities or both. Claim-rights impose duties upon others and immunities impose 'disabilities' or 'no powers' upon others. Both sorts of right are instruments of non-domination. Slavery is the most complete form of domination just because it is a rightless condition. Certainly some – but equally certainly not all – of the rights that theorists like myself champion are rights to non-interference, but to have a *right* to non-interference is quite different from merely *being* not interfered with. According people rights creates precisely the sort of condition that non-domination demands.

Rights and collective goods

Although Bellamy's argument may contain hints of scepticism about rights-talk, he is not hostile to rights as such. For Bellamy, rights can properly figure in a political arrangement provided they do so as the instruments or offspring of democracy rather its rivals. But the extent to which rights now figure in people's political vocabularies does often attract scepticism. Even someone who is broadly sympathetic to a rights-approach has reason to acknowledge that it is not the most defensible or appropriate approach for every issue a society confronts. Healthcare is now frequently talked about in the language of rights, but Albert Weale gives us reason to doubt whether healthcare policy is best conceived in those terms and I can only assent to his measured scepticism.

Weale's scepticism is directed not, of course, at the desirability or goodness of healthcare. Health would seem to be amongst the least controversial of human goods and, even allowing for asceticism, it scores well as a cross-cultural good. Rather his scepticism concerns the utility and appropriateness of a rights-approach to healthcare. As he points out, the right to healthcare is now well entrenched in human rights documents and the International Covenant on Economic, Social and Cultural Rights (ICESCR) (1966) sets the bar high in asserting that everyone has the right to 'the highest attainable standard of physical and mental health' (article 12). Weale's assessment of this right focuses more upon healthcare as a human *right* than as a *human* right, but both claims are controversial.

It seems clear that, in 1948, the drafters of the UDHR did not conceive the socio-economic rights included in the Declaration as genuinely human rights. Rather they conceived them as rights of citizens, that is, as rights that each government or each society should secure for its citizens. The fact that the rights were formulated not as rights to general resources or to a given standard of material well-being but as rights to specific goods and services indicates that they would be primarily rights possessed by individuals as members of states. Indeed, they were clearly rights inspired the welfare states that had developed in many industrialized societies. The UDHR described itself as setting 'a common standard of achievement for all peoples and all nations' and, in line with that self-characterization, the Declaration was partly an exercise in target-setting for governments. Now it could be that states, or their governments, were thought of as mere intermediaries that humanity was using to deliver genuinely universal rights, but I have never been persuaded by that claim. If the goods and services secured to each individual were to be geared to the resources available to each state – and article 22 of the UDHR came clean in stating that the right to social security was to be 'in accordance with the organization and resources of each state' – the socio-economic goods to which the members of poor states were entitled were markedly different and inferior to those claimable by individuals in rich societies. How, then, could these be authentically human rights: rights possessed identically and equally by all human beings as human beings? The human right to healthcare illustrates that objection particularly well. No amount of pleading about the relevance of local circumstances can show that the rights to healthcare that contemporary India or Mali might extend to its citizens can equate in value with those that can be enjoyed in contemporary Switzerland or Sweden.

That is not to say that a human right to healthcare is intrinsically nonsensical. On the contrary, securing an equivalent level of healthcare amongst the world's population is both intelligible and, for the most part and in principle, possible. My point is simply that, if we assert a 'human right' to healthcare, we should mean what we say and conceive the right as a global right with its attendant global obligations and global claims upon resources. Nowadays, a greater number of people than half a century ago are willing to think about socio-economic goods in a genuinely cosmopolitan way, but, beyond the relief of poverty, their views are still not widely shared by either politicians or ordinary citizens.

If we set aside the issue of whether health should be conceived as a genuinely *human* right, we are still left with Weale's question: do rights (of any kind) provide us with the appropriate normative apparatus for thinking about goods such as healthcare? A common complaint is that assertions of rights to socio-economic goods, such as healthcare, provide us with no clue about the specific quantity and quality of the good to which there is a right. The ICESCR may appear to be an exception in asserting a right to the 'highest attainable standard of physical and mental health' (article 12) but, as Weale ably demonstrates, that standard is simply question-begging.

However, Weale's doubts about the serviceability of a general right to healthcare go beyond the common complaint that it fails to answer the question: a right to how much? Rather he argues that we have reason to think about goods such as healthcare in terms other than rights.

He contrasts the rights approach with the beneficial design approach. In some measure, resource issues remain important to the differences between those approaches. If we move from the idea of a universal right to a basic level of healthcare to the goal of 'comprehensive, high quality care available to all those eligible for its services without financial barriers to access' (p. 473), the greater ambition of that goal will mean that the claims of healthcare will compete more fiercely for resources with the claims of other social goods. Moreover, as Weale explains, we shall also be faced with severe choices between competing claims within the category of healthcare. Invoking rights is singularly unhelpful in dealing with those competing claims to resources.

However, the contrast Weale draws is not merely a contrast between the relative utility of two different approaches for resolving issues of scarce resources. It is a contrast between two fundamentally different normative approaches to the provision of healthcare. A rights-based approach will begin with the question, what is the healthcare to which each individual has a right? And it will go on to ask, what are the obligations imposed by that right and upon whom does it impose those obligations? Ultimately, if not immediately, those who bear the obligations are likely to encompass most of those who hold the right; even so, a rights-approach will still give primacy to the demands people can make upon each other. By contrast, the beneficial design approach starts with the question: how should we provide for our healthcare? It asks not what can each of us demand of the rest, but what should we do together? It treats the provision of healthcare as a collective endeavour: what sorts of healthcare arrangement should we put in place to provide for our mutual good? That perspective seems more consonant with the approach to health policy in societies like Britain and also more consonant with a health policy that aims to do more than secure a basic minimum for all. It is also more consistent with the area of discretion we generally suppose each society has in deciding how it should deploy its public resources. As Weale points out, while the beneficial design approach does not start from individual rights, it can issue in rights – rights that give citizens equal access to the healthcare for which their society has made collective provision. For those who aspire to make rights justiciable, the only right to health that has any chance of being assessable by a court is one that has emerged from a series of complex and detailed policy decisions and that is nested within a given set of policy parameters. If the right to healthcare is supposed to lie at the foundation of health policy, judges are clearly not the right people to decide what it demands.

We might tell similar stories about how Weale's two approaches relate to goods such as education, housing, and personal security. In their case too, we are likely to conclude that the assertion of rights is of little help in deciding what sort of provision we should make, and of doubtful merit in determining the moral spirit in which we make that provision. So do we have any reason to go on characterizing healthcare and its like as fundamental rights? One purpose that claims of right, especially claims of human right, have served has been to identify goods that we should prioritize because of their special value for human beings. That purpose has been an important driver behind the addition of socio-economic rights to the traditional catalogues of civil and political rights. If we do not add rights to healthcare or to adequate food, clothing and shelter to the list of human rights, we may appear to be saying that those goods matter less than freedom of expression, freedom of religion and the other standard fare of traditional declarations. In most people's lives, the opposite is likely to be true. Indeed, if we apply Miller's test of what is needed for a minimally decent life, healthcare, along with many other socio-economic goods, scores well and does so for reasons that are much more simple and straightforward than those that argue for freedom of expression or freedom of religion. In so far as we want to go on using the idea of rights to assure a basic minimum to all, either as citizens or as human beings, so that there will be 'bread for all before jam for some', we have reason to go on speaking of healthcare in the language of rights. But, when we turn to the actual provision of goods such as healthcare, we can have reason to aspire to more than the notional minima those rights demand, and reason, as Weale shows, not to expect rights to contribute helpfully to resolving the policy issues we shall encounter. Rights should have an important place in our moral and political thinking, but they should not monopolize either sort of thinking.

The ease with which people can and do assert rights and the consequent proliferation of rights-claims has become a major preoccupation of commentators on rights. For some, it has helped foster a hostility to claims of moral and human rights reminiscent of Jeremy Bentham (e.g. Geuss 2001). For others, it has helped make the case for limiting 'rights' to conventional rights, principally legal rights. For these conventionalists, a 'moral right' should be understood as a morally justified conventional right; in the absence of a conventional right, there simply is no right that can be either moral or immoral (e.g. Darby 2009, Martin 1993). In a similar spirit, many now argue that expansive moral thought on the rights that we might ascribe to human beings should give way to a focus on the political function that human rights actually perform in the contemporary world. The idea of human rights should be shaped by its practical role in justifying international intervention and by the real-world practice of human rights that has developed since 1948 (e.g. Beitz 2009, Rawls 1999, Raz 2010). While there is much to commend these efforts to contain rights thinking within some sort of limit, there is also a danger that they will exclude too much. The idea of moral rights as morally grounded entitlements provides a distinctive and significant element of our moral thinking and, arguably, we have to think of human rights as moral rights first and foremost if they are to perform their traditional role of curbing and containing the use of political power (Jones 2012). But those of us who want to keep faith with the orthodox conceptions of moral and human rights still face a major challenge in setting non-arbitrary boundaries to rights that prevent the orthodoxy collapsing into an anarchy of rights-claims that devalues and discredits the very idea of rights.

Acknowledgements
I am grateful to the participants of the conference at which the papers in this issue were first presented for their thoughts and comments. I am also indebted to Rowan Cruft, Ian O'Flynn and Albert Weale for their helpful advice and comments on an earlier draft of this paper.

Notes
1. This would have been better expressed as telling those who wield political power 'what they may not do to, and what they must do for, those over whom they wield their power'. That formulation would have better captured the point that human rights can impose positive as well as negative obligations on power-holders.
2. I suspect the comment had its origins in arguments I had with Simon Caney over many years on the relative merits of neutralist and perfectionist liberalism. I would always start from the case of religion, while he would always start from the cases of opera and the non-medical use of drugs.
3. I previously assumed too readily that the impartial treatment demanded by fairness must be equal or equivalent treatment. But, even if we hold, for example, that fairness is consistent with greater weight being given to the culture of the indigenous or majority population by comparison with the cultures of migrant groups, that judgement still implies the sort of external or supra-cultural perspective that I go on to describe. Insofar as this view involves a commitment to a general principle that, for some public purposes, an indigenous culture should weigh more than migrant cultures, that principle remains impartial with respect to any particular culture qua particular culture. If, on the other hand, an imbalance in the weight given to the indigenous culture and migrant cultures reflects no more than an imbalance in the power of indigenous and migrant groups, there will be nothing 'impartial' about it.
4. This is an issue to which Bellamy has given a great deal of attention, both normative and empirical (Bellamy 2007). The few doubts I express here do not even begin to address the extensive and closely argued case he makes.

References
Barry, B., 1995. *Justice as impartiality*. Oxford: Clarendon.
Barry, B., 2001. *Culture and equality*. Cambridge: Polity Press.

Beitz, C.R., 2009. *The idea of human rights*. Oxford: Oxford University Press.
Bellamy, R., 2007. *Political constitutionalism: a republican defence of the constitutionality of democracy*. Cambridge: Cambridge University Press.
Curran, C.E., 1998. Churches and human rights: from hostility/reluctance to acceptability. *Milltown Studies*, 42 (Winter), 30–58.
Darby, D., 2009. *Rights, race and recognition*. Cambridge: Cambridge University Press.
Dworkin, R., 1990. Foundations of liberal equality. *In*: G.B. Peterson, ed. *The Tanner Lectures on human values, XI*. Salt Lake City, UT: University of Utah Press, 1–119.
Geuss, R., 2001. *History and illusion in politics*. Cambridge: Cambridge University Press.
Goodin, R. and Reeve, A., 1989. *Liberal neutrality*. London: Routledge.
Jones, P., 1994. *Rights*. Basingstoke: Macmillan.
Jones, P., 1998. Political theory and cultural diversity. *Critical Review of International Social and Political Philosophy*, 1 (1), 28–62.
Jones, P., 2001. Human rights and diverse cultures: continuity or discontinuity? *In*: S. Caney and P. Jones, eds. *Human rights and global diversity*. London: Frank Cass, 27–50.
Jones, P., forthcoming 2012. Moral rights, human rights, and social recognition. *Political Studies*.
Martin, R., 1993. *A system of rights*. Oxford: Clarendon.
Pettit, P., 1997. *Republicanism*. Oxford: Clarendon.
Rawls, J., 1993. *Political liberalism*. New York, NY: Columbia University Press.
Rawls, J., 1999. *The law of peoples*. Cambridge, MA: Harvard University Press.
Raz, J., 2010. Human rights without foundations. *In*: S. Besson and J. Tasioulas, eds. *The philosophy of international law*. Oxford: Oxford University Press, 321–338.
Scanlon, T.M., 1998. *What we owe to each other*. Cambridge, MA: Harvard University Press.
Steiner, H., 1994. *An essay on rights*. Oxford: Blackwell.

Peter Jones: Publications

Legalising toleration: a reply to Balint. *Res Publica*, 18 (2012), DOI: 10.1007/s11158-012-9178-2.

Moral rights, human rights, and social recognition. *Political Studies* (forthcoming).

Toleration. *In*: F. D'Agostino and G. Gaus, eds. *The Routledge companion to social and political philosophy*. London: Routledge (forthcoming).

Toleration, religion and accommodation. *European Journal of Philosophy*, 20 (2012), DOI: 10.1111/j.1468-0378.2012.00549.x.

Can a compromise be fair? *Politics, Philosophy and Economics*, 2012, DOI: 10.1177/1470594X12447773 (co-authored with Ian O'Flynn).

Internal conflict, the international community, and the promotion of principled compromise. *Government and Opposition*, 47 (3) (2012), 395–413 (co-authored with Ian O'Flynn).

Religion, politics and law. *In*: R. Catto and L. Woodhead, eds. *Religion and change in Britain*. London: Routledge, 2012, 299–321 (co-authored with Gladys Ganiel).

Freedom of expression and religious belief: is 'offensiveness' really the issue? *Res Publica*, 17 (1) (2011), 75–90.

Political toleration: a reply to Newey. *British Journal of Political Science*, 41 (2) (2011), 445–447.

The ethics of international society. *In*: D. Bell, ed. *Ethics and world politics*. Oxford: Oxford University Press, 2010, 111–129.

The politics of recognition. *In*: M. Bevir, ed. *Encyclopedia of political theory*. Thousand Oaks, CA: Sage, 2010, 1076–1078.

Toleration and recognition: what should we teach? *Educational Philosophy and Theory*, 42 (1) (2010), 38–56.

Cultures, group rights and group-differentiated rights. *In*: M. Dimova-Cookson and P. Stirk, eds. *Multiculturalism and moral conflict*. London: Routledge, 2009, 38–57.

Group rights. Aldershot: Ashgate, 2009.

International toleration and the 'War on Terror'. *Globalizations*, 6 (1) (2009), 37–51.

Can speech be intolerant? *In*: G. Newey, ed. *Freedom of expression: counting the costs*. Newcastle: Cambridge Scholars, 2008, 9–29.

Group rights. *In: Stanford encyclopedia of philosophy* (2008). Available from: http://plato.stanford.edu/.

Tolleranza internazionale ed eguale rispetto. *In*: I. Carter and V. Ottonelli, eds. *Eguale rispetto*. Milan: Bruno Mondadori, 2008, 174–200.

Human rights. *In*: E. Craig, ed. *Routledge encyclopedia of philosophy online*. London: Routledge, 2007.

Making sense of political toleration. *British Journal of Political Science*, 37 (3) (2007), 383–402.

Equality, recognition and difference. *Critical Review of International, Social and Political Philosophy*, 9 (1) (2006), 23–46.

Toleration, recognition and identity. *Journal of Political Philosophy*, 14 (2) (2006), 123–143.

Toleration, value pluralism, and the fact of pluralism. *Critical Review of International, Social and Political Philosophy*, 9 (2) (2006), 189–210.

Law and disobedience. *Res Publica*, 10 (4) (2004), 319–336.

Toleration and neutrality: compatible ideals? *In*: D. Castiglione and C. MacKinnon, eds. *Toleration, democracy and neutrality*. Dordrecht: Kluwer, 2003, 97–110.

Disagreement and difference. *Critical Review of International, Social and Political Philosophy*, 6 (3) (2003), 1–11 (co-authored with Simon Caney).

Freedom. *In*: P. B. Clarke and J. Fowraker, eds. *Encyclopedia of democratic thought*. London: Routledge, 2001, 293–298.

with Simon Caney, eds. *Human rights and global diversity*. London: Frank Cass, 2001.

Global distributive justice. *In*: A. Valls, ed. *Ethics and international affairs: theories and cases*. Lanham, MD: Rowman & Littlefield, 2000, 169–184.

Human rights and diverse cultures: continuity or discontinuity? *Critical Review of International, Social and Political Philosophy*, 3 (1) (2000), 27–50.

Individuals, communities and human rights. *Review of International Studies*, 26 (5) (2000), 199–125.

International justice – amongst whom? *In*: T. Coates, ed. *International justice*. Aldershot: Avebury, 2000, 111–129.

Beliefs and identities. *In*: J. Horton and S. Mendus, eds. *Toleration, identity and difference*. London: Macmillan, 1999, 65–86.

Group rights and group oppression. *Journal of Political Philosophy*, 7 (4) (1999), 353–377.

Human rights, group rights, and peoples' rights. *Human Rights Quarterly*, 21 (1) (1999), 80–107.

Commentary on Steiner and McGovern [on Free Trade]. *In*: G. Parry, A. Qureshi and H. Steiner, eds. *The legal and moral aspects of free trade*. London: Routledge, 1998, 218–220.

Freedom of speech. *In*: E. Craig, ed. *Routledge encyclopedia of philosophy*. London: Routledge, 1998, vol. 3, 762–765.

Human rights and diversity of value. *Milltown Studies*, 42 (Winter) (1998), 117–145.

Political theory and cultural diversity. *Critical Review of International, Social and Political Philosophy*, 1 (1) (1998), 28–62.

International human rights: philosophical or political? *In*: S. Caney, D. George and P. Jones, eds. *National rights, international obligations.* Boulder, CO: Westview, 1996, 183–204.

National rights, international obligations. Boulder, CO: Westview, 1996 (co-edited with Simon Caney and David George).

Hugh Berrington: a profile and an appreciation. *In*: P. Jones, ed. *Party, parliament and personality: essays presented to Hugh Berrington.* London: Routledge, 1995, 11–21.

Members of Parliament and issues of conscience. *In*: P. Jones, ed. *Party, parliament and personality: essays presented to Hugh Berrington.* London: Routledge, 1995, 141–164.

On dealing fairly with cultural diversity. *In*: J. Lovenduski and J. Stanyer, eds. *Contemporary political studies 1995.* York: Political Studies Association, 1995, vol. 1, 73–79.

Party, parliament and personality: essays presented to Hugh Berrington. London: Routledge, 1995.

Two conceptions of liberalism, two conceptions of justice. *British Journal of Political Science*, 25 (4) (1995), 515–550.

Bearing the consequences of belief. *Journal of Political Philosophy*, 2 (1) (1994), 24–43.

Rights. Basingstoke: Macmillan, 1994.

The *Satanic Verses* and the politics of identity. *In*: M Fletcher, ed. *Reading Rushdie.* Amsterdam: Rodopi, 1994, 321–333.

Toleration, the Rushdie affair and the perils of identity. *Synthesis Philosophica*, 9 (1) (1994), 27–40.

Evaluation. *In*: M. Harrop, ed. *Power and policy in liberal democracies.* Cambridge: Cambridge University Press, 1992, 241–262.

Respecting beliefs and rebuking Rushdie. *British Journal of Political Science*, 20 (4) (1990), 415–437.

Rushdie, race and religion. *Political Studies*, 38 (4) (1990), 687–694.

Universal principles and particular claims: from welfare rights to welfare states. *In*: R. Goodin and A. Ware, eds. *Needs and welfare.* London: Sage, 1990, 34–53.

Liberalism, belief and doubt. *In*: R. Bellamy, ed. *Liberalism and recent legal and social philosophy.* ARSP, Beiheft 36. Stuttgart: Steiner, 1989, 51–69.

Re-examining rights. *British Journal of Political Science*, 19 (1) (1989), 69–96.

The ideal of the neutral state. *In*: R. Goodin and A. Reeve, eds. *Liberal neutrality.* London: Routledge, 1989, 9–38.

Intense preferences, strong beliefs and democratic decision-making. *Political Studies*, 36 (1) (1988), 7–29.

Toleration, harm and moral effect. *In*: J. Horton and S. Mendus, eds. *Aspects of toleration*. London: Methuen, 1985, 136–157.

Democracy and freedom of expression. *Philosopher*, October (1983), 31–36.

Political equality and majority rule. *In*: D. Miller and L. Siedentop, eds. *The nature of political theory*. Oxford: Clarendon, 1983, 155–182.

with Robert Sugden, Evaluating choice: a reply. *International Review of Law and Economics*, 3 (1) (1983), 85–87.

Freedom and the redistribution of resources. *Journal of Social Policy*, 11 (2) (1982), 217–238.

Evaluating choice. *International Review of Law and Economics*, 2 (1) (1982), 47–65 (co-authored with Robert Sugden).

Blasphemy, offensiveness and law. *British Journal of Political Science*, 10 (2) (1980), 129–148.

Rights, welfare and stigma. *In*: N. Timms, ed. *Social welfare: why and how?* London: Routledge & Kegan Paul, 1980, 123–144.

Index

Note:
reference 40n14 refers to note 14 on page 40

adversarial circumstances 11–12
Anscombe, E. 99
Arendt, H. 67
Arneson, R. 51
arrest or detention, arbitrary 34
arts 46–7; opera 4–5, 36, 42, 43, 46–8, 53–7, 114–15
association, freedom of 31, 33, 34–5
autonomy 21–2, 25, 26, 49, 63, 71

Backman, G. 86
Barry, B. 46, 48–9, 51, 115, 118
Battin, M.P. 102
Beccaria, C. 69
Beitz, C.R. 126
Belgium 115
Bellamy, R. 63, 64, 65, 68, 69, 73, 75, 79, 81, 91, 119
beneficial design discourse *see* right to health versus good medical care
Bentham, J. 2
Bevan, Aneurin 90
bias: status quo 78; *see also* individualistic bias of rights
bills of rights 62–3, 65, 80
blasphemy 116
blood transfusions 32
bodily integrity, right to 32, 38
Brownlie, I. 34, 35, 88

Canada 115
cancer: anti-cancer pharmaceuticals 95; National Institute for Health and Clinical Excellence (NICE) 96–7
capabilities 39n8
Catholic Church 109–10
charity 14–15
children 88, 89

Christianity 3, 53, 54, 109–10, 116, 117–18
Church of England 53, 54, 116, 117–18
circumcision, female 38
claim-rights 123
Colombia 87
commercial organizations 114
common or public good 6–7, 69–70, 71, 76; courts 79–80
compossible/incompossible 12, 16, 68, 100
concern and respect, equal 63, 67, 69, 70, 71, 72, 74, 75, 76, 79, 120
conscience, freedom of 23, 32, 34–5, 38, 111
constitutional courts 5, 73, 75, 77, 78–9, 87
constitutional and everyday politics 5, 73, 74
continuous approach 2–3, 10, 109–10
cost-effectiveness 95–100, 101–2, 103–4
courts 5, 63, 73, 74–5, 97, 122; and editorial democracy 74, 80–1; equity 80; fair trial 23, 35–6, 79, 89, 92, 94, 97–8, 111, 113, 118; judicial review 73, 74, 75, 77–81, 87, 121; procedural fairness 80; as unreal democracy 76–80
Curran, C.E. 110

Darby, D. 126
deadlock 12–13
death penalty 68
democracy 5, 38, 109–10, 117; electoral competition between parties 75; famines and 40n14; majority rule 5, 75, 117; party manifestos and government policies 75; Rawls 51; rights as *see separate entry*; state

INDEX

neutrality 42, 47–8, 49, 54; subsidies to arts 47–8, 54, 56
detention, arbitrary 34
developing societies 89
dignity 92–3
disability 86
disagreement: doctrinal 10–14, 18, 22, 110, 111; majority rule 75; rights 5–6, 62–3, 64–5, 68–9, 76, 77, 119
discontinuous approach 3, 4, 5, 10–11, 109–10, 114, 117
discrimination 111; equal right to protection against 35; right to health 86
diseases 103; contagious 89
diversity of value and human rights 3–4, 9–10, 21–4, 37–8; doctrinal neutrality 10–14, 16, 18; equal freedom 15–18; moral primacy 14–15, 16, 18, 110; reply 108–11; state neutrality implausible and unnecessary *see separate entry*
Dworkin, R 10, 46–7, 63, 77, 89, 98, 109

education 29, 30, 57, 126; religious 28, 29, 30
Ely, J.H. 77, 78
employers 88
Enlightenment 3
environmental protection 89
equal freedom 15–18
equal recognition 55
equal respect 51, 55–6; rights as democracy 63, 67, 69, 70, 71, 72, 74, 75, 76, 79, 120
equality and liberals 35
European Convention on Human Rights 121; health 88
expression, freedom of 23, 31, 33, 34–5, 68, 69–70, 78, 118, 126

fair share, right to health as right to *see* right to health versus good medical care
fair trial 23, 35–6, 79, 89, 92, 94, 97–8, 111, 113, 118
famines and democracy 40n14
female circumcision 38
Finland 75
first level of concern 3, 11, 15, 22
food, clothing and shelter 126
France 90
free speech/freedom of expression 23, 31, 33, 34–5, 68, 69–70, 78, 118, 126

freedom 4, 50, 92, 109
freedom allocations, rights as 9–10; doctrinal neutrality 10–14, 16, 18; equal freedom 15–18; moral primacy 14–15, 16, 18, 110
freedom as non-interference 64, 81; liberalism, rights and 67–70, 122–3
freedom/liberty as non-domination 63, 64, 67, 75, 76, 81, 120, 121–3; republicanism, rights and 70–3
Freeman, M. 86
Freeman, S. 48
friendship and love, needs for 33, 112

George, H. 16
Geuss, R. 126
Gewirth, A. 16
Goddin, R. 108
good and rights, conceptions of the 2–4, 42, 46, 50, 57, 114–16; discontinuous approach 3, 4, 5, 10–11, 109–10, 114, 117; grounding human rights *see separate entry*; 'reasonable pluralism' 3; *see also* diversity of value and human rights; state neutrality implausible and unnecessary
governments: political power and human rights 2, 5, 23–4, 62, 67, 113–14, 118, 127
Griffin, J. 94
grounding human rights 4, 21–4, 37–8, 110–11; capabilities 39n8; human needs proper and societal needs 26–30, 37; margin of appreciation 33; monistic approach 24, 112–13; needs, human 25–38; 'overlapping consensus' strategy 24; overshoot problem 25, 30–3, 37; pluralistic approach 24–5, 26, 36–7, 111–12, 113; reply 111–14; undershoot problem 25–6, 33–7
Guantanamo Bay detention centre 27

Habermas, J. 73, 77, 78, 119
Hadorn, D.C. 102
Hart, H.L.A. 9, 10, 11, 16–18, 104
hate speech 69
health and safety, occupational 88, 89
healthcare 23; global inequalities 94–5; grounding human rights on needs 30, 31–2; international law: declarations of right to health 87–8; right to health versus good medical care *see separate entry*
Hobbes, T. 92, 119, 123

INDEX

Hohfeld, W.N. 14, 17, 64–5, 122–3
holidays with pay, right to periodic 34
homeless persons 93
Horton, J. 51, 115
housing 101, 126
humanitarian intervention 24

immunities 122, 123
incitement 69
incompossible/compossible 12, 16, 68, 100
indigenous peoples 86
individualistic bias of rights 2, 6, 37–8; *see also* right to health versus good medical care
Interest Theory of rights 18
International Covenant on Economic, Social and Cultural Rights (ICESCR) 88, 123, 124
international human rights conventions 62–3, 65
intimidation 69
Islam 53, 109, 116

Jehovah's Witnesses 32
Jones, P. 1, 2, 3, 5, 9–11, 13–14, 15–16, 18, 21–3, 24, 25, 37–8, 41–6, 47, 49–53, 55, 61–3, 64–5, 66, 67, 71, 81, 86, 87, 92, 93, 102, 104, 110, 113, 117, 121, 127
judicial review 73, 74, 75, 77–81, 87, 121

Kant, I. 16
Kavanagh, A. 77
Klingermann, H.-D. 75
Kukathas, C. 46
Kymlicka, W. 46

language 115
legal procedure rights 23
levels of concern 3, 11, 14, 15, 22, 110
libel 69
liberal neutrality *see* state neutrality implausible and unnecessary
liberalism, perfectionist 49
liberalism, rights and freedom as non-interference 67–70, 122–3
liberties to act 14, 64–5
liberty, right to 29–30, 92
liberty/freedom as non-domination 63, 64, 67, 75, 76, 81, 121–3; republicanism, rights and 70–3
life, right to 88, 92

litigation 63, 73–5, 76–81; form of participation 73, 77, 79
Locke, J. 16, 42, 67, 71, 92
love and friendship, needs for 33, 112

MacCormick, N. 16
McGann, A.J. 76
MacIntyre, A. 50
margin of appreciation 33
Maritain, J. 3
Martin, R. 114, 126
Marxism 111
May, K. 66
mental illness 86
Menzel, P. 102
Mill, J.S. 62
Miller, D. 15, 50, 110, 112, 113
minimally decent human life *see* needs, grounding human rights on
moral primacy 14–15, 16, 18, 110
movement, freedom of 31, 33
Muslims/Islam 53, 109, 116

Nagel, T. 51
nationalism 111
nationality 113
natural disasters 24
natural law 3
natural rights 1–2, 10, 16, 17–18, 19n2, 23, 62, 64, 65, 67, 71, 72, 81, 86, 92, 111, 113–14, 123
needs, grounding human rights on 4, 21–5, 37–8, 110–11; human needs proper and societal needs 26–30, 37; margin of appreciation 33; overshoot problem 25, 30–3, 37; reply 111–14; undershoot problem 25–6, 33–7
negative rights: costs 97–8
neutrality 108–11; doctrinal 10–14, 16, 18; languages 115; state neutrality implausible and unnecessary *see separate entry*
New Zealand 79
non-democratic states 72–3, 120
non-domination 63, 64, 67, 75, 76, 81, 120, 121–3; republicanism, rights and freedom as 70–3
non-interference 14, 63, 64, 81; demarcation of domains 13; human needs and bodily integrity 32; liberalism, rights and freedom as 67–70, 122–3
Norway 75, 90
Nozick, R. 91, 92

INDEX

nutrition 89

Obama, Barack 89
official secrets 69
O'Neill, O. 69, 89
opera 4–5, 36, 42, 43, 46–8, 53–7, 114–15
opportunity cost 99
Ordeshook, P.C. 75
organ transplants 32

Paine, T. 3
perfectionist liberalism 49
personal security, right to 29–30, 92, 94, 111, 113, 126
Pettit, P. 63, 67, 71, 74, 80, 122
pharmaceutical drugs 90, 94–5
Plato 116
pluralistic approach 24–5, 26, 36–7, 111–12, 113
police 92
political power and human rights 2, 5, 23–4, 62, 67, 113–14, 118, 127
political representation, right to 35–6
politics, constitutional and everyday 5, 73, 74
Pollock, L. 16
poverty 24, 124
precedent 78
primacy, moral 14–15, 16, 18, 110
prison sentences 29–30
privacy law 121
property rights 66, 72
proportional representation 79
proportionality 77, 80
public or common good 6–7, 69–70, 71, 76; courts 79–80
public expenditure: subsidies to opera or arts more generally 4–5, 42, 43, 46–8, 53–7, 114–15

quality-adjusted life-year (QALY) 96–7, 101–2

Rawls, J. 3, 9–10, 42–3, 47–8, 51, 65, 73, 77, 94, 98, 102, 109–10, 119, 126
Raz, J. 49, 66, 69, 89, 126
recognition: equal 55; need for 35, 36; as person before the law 35, 36
Reeve, A. 108
refugees 93, 101
religion 38, 47, 109–10; blasphemy 116; Christianity 3, 53, 54, 109–10, 116, 117–18; education 28, 29, 30; established church 53, 54; freedom of 38, 111, 113, 116, 126; Jehovah's Witnesses 32; Muslims/Islam 53, 109, 116; observance 29
remedy, right to effective 35, 36
republicanism, rights and freedom as non-domination 70–3
respect, equal 51, 55–6; rights as democracy 63, 67, 69, 70, 71, 72, 74, 75, 76, 79, 120
right to health versus good medical care 85–7, 103–4; charges and no financial barriers to access 90; cost-effectiveness requirements 95–100; defining the incompatibility 87–91; enhancement or healthcare 90; expansion of content of right 92; opportunity cost 99; primary good 93–4; quality-adjusted life-year (QALY) 96–7, 101–2; reply 123–7; right to health as right to fair share 100–3; rights as grounds 91–5; social and political equality 93
rights as democracy 5–6, 61–4, 81; authorial merits of real democracy 74–6; courts as editorial democracy 74, 80–1; courts as unreal democracy 76–80; non-democratic states 72–3, 120; reply 118–23; rights and democracy: real and ideal 73–81; rights and individual liberty: liberal and republican perspectives 67–73; rights, political equality and democracy 64–7; stateless persons or citizens of different state 72–3
Roman Catholic Church 109–10
Rueda, P. 87

Sacks, Sir Jonathan 53
sanitation 89, 95
Scanlon, T.M. 112
second-order device 3, 11, 14, 22, 110
security, right to personal 29–30, 92, 94, 111, 113, 126
Sikora, K. 97
Skinner, Q. 63
slander 69
slavery 34, 123
social contact 31, 33, 34–5
social contract 92; healthcare 87, 91, 92, 103–4
social security 113

socio-economic rights 23, 77, 87, 97, 111, 112, 123–4, 126; healthcare *see separate entry*
sovereignty 72
Spencer, H. 16
state neutrality implausible and unnecessary 4–5, 41–6, 56–7; basic structure approach 46, 47–9; conceptions of impartiality 46; equal respect 51, 55–6; perfectionist liberalism 49; reply 114–18; special pleading approach 46–7; strategy allows people to live according to own cultures 46, 54–5; strategy must not be drawn from any particular culture 46, 50–2; strategy must not seek to privilege any particular culture 46, 52–4; subsidies to opera or arts more generally 4–5, 42, 43, 46–8, 53–7, 114–15
stateless persons 72–3
Steiner, H. 12, 15, 16, 18, 55, 100, 109, 110
subsidies to opera or arts more generally 4–5, 42, 43, 46–8, 53–7, 114–15
subsistence, right to 35–6

Tasioulas, J. 26
taxation 54, 55
Taylor, C. 55
titles, rights as 93
tortured, right not to be 5, 34, 61, 68–9, 88, 89, 97, 111, 118
travellers 93
Tushnet, M. 76

United Kingdom 75, 79, 125; Human Rights Act 81; National Health Service 90, 96; National Institute for Health and Clinical Excellence (NICE) 96–7; quality-adjusted life-year (QALY) 96–7
United Nations 100, 101; Convention Relating to the Status of Refugees 101; Covenant on Economic, Social and Cultural Rights 88, 123, 124; Declaration of Human Rights 34, 35, 85, 87–8, 92–3, 113, 121, 123–4; Declaration of the Rights of the Child 88; Special Rapporteur on right to health 86
United States 5; death penalty 68; Guantanamo Bay detention centre 27; healthcare 89; judicial review 75, 79
utilitarianism 52, 102

vaccination 89
vote, right to 5, 33, 61, 79, 118

Waldron, J. 14, 18, 65, 72
water supply 89, 95
Weale, A. 31, 50, 65, 90, 124
White, J. 91
Will Theory of rights 16–18
Williams, Rowan 116
Wolff, J. 94
women 38, 72, 79, 114
work 29; clean and safe workplace 88
wrong, right to do 14–15